The Essential Social Marketing Bundle

Marketing Bundle
(2 Books in 1)

J. E. Ford

Book 1:

Social Media Marketing for the Future:

Strategies for 2020 & Beyond

J. E. Ford

Overview

There are few things in the 21st Century that have been as revolutionary as the development of social media. Still in many ways in its infancy, the scope and field of social media has changed so much since its birth. As with most powerful forces in society, money is one of the most significant motivators that drives change in the social media realm. The amount of money that is in play and under the control of powerhouses like Facebook and YouTube is staggering. For virtually every business out there, social media plays a role in their industry, audience, and market reach whether they realize it or not. Social Media Marketing is no longer an experimental advertising tool used by very specific types of companies. Social Media Marketing is no longer optional. With over 75% of people active on Social Media, and with the decline in performance of other advertising and marketing methods, Social Media Marketing is often your best chance of reaching your customers.

However, things are not fixed in social media. Things are changing. Just as the platforms and the way people use them are still being established, laws and regulations are also evolving to be more relevant for digital marketing. This fluidity and rapid rate of change makes it difficult to keep abreast of digital marketing trends and patterns. Once you invest your time and resources into building a social media presence based on conventional input, your marketing strategy may already be outdated. An effective social media marketers will understand the importance of adapting and flexing with the pervasive change and not only will they be able to react to changes in the market, but they will be looking ahead and planning their marketing strategy according to the changes that are coming. This will help them stay relevant to their customers and stay ahead of their competitors.

Paradoxically, the best way to beat the competition is to do what they aren't doing. Most companies are way behind the curve when it comes to social media marketing and digital marketing strategies. They are only now getting up to speed with strategies that are already outdated. Large corporations and companies that have been around for a long time are at a distinct disadvantage because they are slower to change. They have a lot of moving pieces and parts that make change more complex. Small companies and startups can be more nimble and have a competitive advantage in many ways when it comes to social media. There are already many resources out there that will help you develop a brand and there are indeed many perennial rules of marketing that apply to social media marketing just as much as they applied to print advertising 20 years ago. However, everyone is playing catch up. All of the marketing resources and books out there are seeking to help you make sense of what's already happened. They're trying to help you take advantage of industry trends that have already matured. You can be sure your competition is already doing the same thing. Your customers are already on to the next thing and before you know it, your methods seem antiquated.

This book seeks to help you develop a future-oriented social media marketing mastery plan. You will learn how to decipher the existing and historical patterns in the industry, how to apply timeless marketing rules to new mediums and technologies, and, most importantly, what the most important future marketing trends are going to be and what they mean for your business.

You will learn about the future of Facebook, Instagram, LinkedIn, Youtube and Snapchat—as well as new platforms you may not be familiar with. You will be able to profile and understand the next generation of consumers that is already at your doorstep.

Educating yourself on what is coming will allow your company to flex and adapt where it needs to, to meet the new demand and reach your customers the way they want to be reached. You will be miles ahead of your customers who are still trying to play catch-up with digital marketing trends that are not sustainable. The playing field has never been more level. You have never had more opportunity to get ahead of the curve and take out the competition with intuition, foresight and willingness to plan for the future.

The future is here. Are you ready for it?

Introduction:

Congratulations on purchasing *Social Media Marketing for the Future* and thank you for doing so. What was once an optional means of reaching out to a small, and frequently young, segment of the market has ballooned into a trillion-dollar industry that is often the key determining factor as to whether a new business lives or dies. Social media marketing has changed dramatically in a short period of time and shows no signs of slowing down.

This level of change makes it difficult to pin down what needs to be done to stay up to date with social media marketing, especially for those who are still getting the hang of the entire process in the first place. Difficult is not impossible, however, which is why the following chapters will discuss everything you need to know in order to get started building a social media marketing plan that you can be relatively confident will last for years to come with minimal alterations. First, you will learn about the predicted future of many of today's social media stalwarts including Facebook, Instagram, LinkedIn, Twitter and YouTube.

From there, you will learn all about Vero, an on the rise social media platform that experts believe may be ready to reach the big leagues. You will then learn about anticipated social media marketing trends in the future as well as those surrounding government regulation, email marketing, and privacy. Finally, you will find tips on cultivating a unique presence as well as a profile of the future of target audiences in the form of Generation Z.

There are plenty of books on this subject on the market,

however, very few, if any, are dedicated to discussing trends for the future to help you come up with a strategy that will put you ahead of the curve and keep you well ahead of your competition. That is what this book is all about. Every effort was made to ensure it is full of as much useful information as possible; please enjoy!

Chapter 1: From the Past to the Future

Over the past decade, social media as a whole has transformed from something isolated to web browsers to a hundred billion dollar industry that more than half the world's population is accessing in some form every single day. With such a dramatic framework already in place, it is only natural to expect the next five years to be full of even more significant growth in the space. Thanks to ongoing advancements in internet infrastructure, the wired and wireless networks (and associated hardware) that make social media possible, the world is only growing more connected than ever before.

The end result will be a sort of changing of the guard in the remaining industries that have not yet felt the impact of social media as well as an even greater social media presence in the average person's life. Despite the fact that the history of social media dictates that something new comes along every few years, many of the platforms discussed in this book have withstood the test of time and, while they are unlikely to reign supreme forever, it is a safe bet they all have a few more years of life in them before they go the way of Friendster and LiveJournal. It also seems evident that some of the trends are here to stay.

While there are new social networks working to rise to prominence all of the time, with more than one discussed in the following chapters, it is important to keep in mind that the current crop of social media all-stars have reach and demographics that their predecessors could only dream of. YouTube, for example, is a direct rival to Netflix, the largest content distribution system on the planet. While something new will ultimately come along, for now, you will see more new startups in the space finding ways to work with these major players as opposed to finding ways to usurp them.

When taken as a whole, the improving dynamics of ever-increasing internet speeds, an app-filled social media landscape and billions of connected always-online devices, it is virtually guaranteed that the next five years will see continued shifts to cultural stalwarts akin to the changes that have come to print, television, and radio over the past decade. As more and more devices that track some form of personal data continue to become more prominent, behavioral shifts are becoming evident with a growing acceptance of the monitoring of personal information, as long as it is at the user's discretion.

While there are always going to be unexpected trends, people and products that dictate where the future of social media takes us, the overarching themes of the democratization of media, portable identity and connectivity will continue to be the primary motivators they always have been. As long as this is the case, it is a safe assumption that the social media landscape of the future will be one that is much expanded, but nevertheless markedly similar, to the social media landscape of today. However, the way in which people conduct business via social media could be dramatically altered. That's what this book seeks to discuss.

The ROI of Social Media Marketing:

For as long as social media has been a household phrase, those in the marketing world have been talking about its ROI (return on investment). Brands have definitely gotten smarter about social media in the past decade, with early adopters driving the conversation and seeing standout profits as a result as the old arguments that social media cannot be used for sales or profit have long since fallen by the wayside. Another facet of this is due to the fact that the social media platforms themselves went and developed business models, varying tiers of advertising and plenty of ways for hungry brands to drive their sales as a result.

Nevertheless, when it comes to ensuring your social media marketing is successful in the long-term, it is essential to look at more than just pure ROI and instead consider the following:

- Driving Sales and Leads
- Driving Research and Development
- Facilitating Customer Service
- Enhancing Public Relations
- Building Community
- Protecting Your Reputation
- Branding and Awareness

These are the areas that can most easily be used to generate viable business goals based on social media marketing. The strategic goal for leveraging a successful social media campaign may be to improve awareness of a given brand or product, or it might be to improve your social media following in general. It could also be used to drive leads through the use of things like webinars and white paper offered up through the most appropriate social media channel.

Regardless of the strategic reasons you choose for utilizing social media marketing, your objectives and goals are always going to have specific outputs, not all of which will be financially motivated. Instead, it makes more sense to measure goals through different criteria such as: the number of negative versus positive search returns when your brand is searched on Google, Q-scores, online sentiment or merely protecting your brand's reputation. While more challenging to measure in some ways, this return can be just as valuable as a purely monetary return.

If you are interested in community building, then measuring the size and scope of the community is a good choice. You could also measure the difference in spending between those who are in the community and everyone else. If you are measuring public relations, on the other hand, then you may want to measure things like the number of key community partners you are engaging with, positive media relation hits and the like to determine the true return of your marketing actions. It is also possible to measure revenue that is generated from new products or features that were generated based on community feedback.

When looking at all of these business drivers, it becomes much easier to see that sales revenue is only one of the outputs that matter and can be broadly connected to several others. Likewise, ROI can certainly be derived from social media, as long as you know what goals to look for. In the end, ROI is just a mathematical equation which means you can count on it to remain the same no matter what. It is simply the difference between the amount of money you spent and the amount of money you made as a result of that expense and marketing activity. If the result is positive then the ROI was worthwhile; otherwise, it is a loss. The end result is most often expressed as a percentage.

When looked at it in this way, measuring social media ROI becomes much more straightforward. All you need to do is look for a holistic approach while at the same time resisting the urge to ignore the soft benefits and metrics that come along with most social media marketing. Most people completely miss the boat here. They get completely caught up in the reporting and added features and benefits that you can often get for free through plug-ins and extensions, and they don't focus enough on the cold hard ROI of their social media marketing expenses and efforts. For those efforts that have the goal of driving revenue, you measure that and calculate an ROI, but know that ROI is not for social marketing overall, but rather for that singular effort. To find success in this field, it is important to focus on the broader return inherent in social media, not just its pure ROI.

Tips for success

While the possibilities are endless when it comes to the future of marketing via social media, there are a few stalwart principles that will never go out of fashion. Keeping them in mind will help you reap results in the short-term while at the same time successfully planning for the long-term.

Try the 80/20 principle: Also known as the Pareto principle, the 80/20 principle is a simple ratio that explains the idea that 80 percent of your results come from 20 percent of your effort. This is a common refrain among sales teams but is equally true of many languages, including English. 20 percent of the words are repeated 80 percent of the time; it is the same with pop music. This principle can be applied to learning if you first take the time to understand with reasonable surety what the most important 20 percent of a topic is. Again, it is important to only apply this principle when you can be more than 75 percent sure you understand what the most important 20 percent of a topic to be. Remember, a little knowledge is a dangerous thing.

In today's hectic, "instant-gratification" world, multitasking has become the norm. The word multitasking is actually a bit of a misnomer as it actually refers to a process whereby you rapidly shift your attention between multiple tasks. When it comes to learning new information, this is absolutely the worst thing you can do as it is important to focus on the new information as completely as possible in order to increase the odds of retaining the information. Rapidly switching focus is one of the easiest ways to ensure you won't be retaining much information and anything you do retain won't be sticking around for long.

Use SMART Goals

Regardless of what you are trying to accomplish, setting clear goals for yourself will help to motivate you to actually follow through on them. When it comes to choosing the right goals, ensuring the ones you choose are SMART is always a good choice.

Specific: Good goals are specific which means you want to be sure that the goal you choose is extremely clear, especially when you are first starting out, as goals that are less well defined are much easier to avoid doing in favor of activities that provide more positive stimulation in a shorter period of time. Keeping specific goals in mind will instead make it much easier for you to go ahead and power through whatever task you are currently undertaking.

Measured: In addition to being specific, you want the goal that you ultimately land on to be one where progress can easily be measured as you go along. Not only will this help you to more easily stay on track throughout the entire process, but it will also make the overall change easier to attain as it will be done in incremental pieces that you can feel good about completing every single time. This incremental process will help allow you to create the types of new neural pathways that you are looking for as they are the first step to creating the types of positive patterns that promote change that you are looking for.

Attainable: SMART goals are those that are attainable given a realistic amount of effort. When it comes to social media marketing, your goal shouldn't be to put yourself in a situation where a large group is going to be focused exclusively on you at first, as that is asking too much of yourself. Instead, a better choice would be to set a goal such as making five conversions in a week. In addition to not picking something too difficult, it is important that you don't lean too far in the other direction and pick something that you can do without any real effort. Goals that are too easily attainable won't do anything to improve your social media marketing skills overall.

Relevant: It is important that the goal you choose is relevant to your current situation as well as being something that is attainable with only a reasonable amount of effort. Relevance is key to turning the SMART goal system from a one-time thing into a pattern and eventually a life-long habit that you can rely on to help you meet the challenges of life no matter what they may be. Remember, you want these early goals to be as meaningful as possible so that you think back on them regularly and fortify the neural pathways as quickly as possible so they become your brain's default way of acting.

Timely: SMART goals are those that have a clear deadline attached. Goals that don't have a clear timeframe for completion are goals that are less likely to ever be completed. Without a clear timetable, you can easily push off what you know you need to do indefinitely. Setting a timeframe will force you to actually confront what it is you want to do and work towards it. The timeframe you choose should be enough to make you hustle, but it doesn't need to be so tight that it is unrealistic.

Chapter 2: The Future of Facebook

Regardless of how you look at it, Facebook is one of the most successful companies of all time. Despite only being in existence for less than 20 years it is already one of the five biggest companies on the planet with a total estimated worth of about $450 billion and more daily users than any other social media platform. With that being said, it is important to keep in mind that July 2018 marked the first time in three years that the company failed to meet user and revenue predictions. Likewise, the 185 million users in Canada and the United States combined remained flat for the first part of the year, and overall additions were at their lowest point since 2011.

In some ways, this is hardly a surprise as Facebook can only grow so far after a certain point, and the scandals that the company has been involved in haven't been much help. Finally, Facebook front man Mark Zuckerberg had previously expressed his opinion that the changes the company was making to improve its News Feed would naturally reduce overall growth as well.

Decidedly profitable

Ad space to spare: Nevertheless, the fact remains that of the three billion people who currently have access to Facebook nearly 75 percent use it on a regular basis which means that devoting time to

Facebook-based advertising is still going to be a worthwhile value proposition. It doesn't matter if you are looking to target an individual group or a wide swath of the market, Facebook has the data to make this type of transaction a reality. In fact, thanks to its mobile app, Facebook is actually the largest overall seller of display advertising in direct competition to Google's previous hold on this position.

Bots: Facebook recently began allowing companies to create bots which are automated lines of code that can be used from within the Facebook Messenger app to allow users to do a wide variety of activities such as find out the weather and even buy everything from food to flowers. The bot interface is surprisingly straightforward, and many of the bots react in much the same way a person would, albeit with a list of responses that are programmed by the developer so the conversation rarely gets off topic.

For example, the bot for 1800 Flowers provides you with the opportunity to buy flowers as well as reach out to customer support directly. You can enter all of your relevant delivery details as well as additional options. While more and more companies are releasing their own apps, there is still room in the space for a number of stalwarts which will reap the rewards of a new community when things ultimately settle down. While there is certainly nothing stopping users from performing these functions outside of the app, the fact that it doesn't require interacting with any unique interfaces should be seen as a significant benefit.

Increasing reliance on video: While there is no denying that both watching and sharing video is extremely popular on Facebook, the site is currently working to ensure that this is an even larger part of the overall experience. In fact, it is now possible to stream live video from virtually any device, even a wide variety of drones.

Improving algorithm:

The fact that Facebook can tell who else is in a picture with you is nothing new, what is new is that soon its software will be capable of recognizing virtually anything that happens inside the picture in question thanks to advanced artificial intelligence algorithms. This will ultimately let users search any of their uploaded pictures using general search terms regardless of whether or not they tagged the photo with the identifier in the first place. This technology is based on the same deep-learning software that powers Google Photos which means this service might be coming to Facebook sooner rather than later.

This technology will ultimately be used to help categorize all of the live video that Facebook anticipates hosting in the near future. This means users will eventually be able to do a search for their favorite sports team, for example, and pull up all of the live video that is currently being streamed that has to do with the team in question.

Facebook VR:

Facebook is already heavily invested in the virtual reality space as it owns the Oculus Rift, one of the premier virtual reality systems on the market, as well as a portion of the Gear VR which is developed by Samsung for use with Smartphone technology. While the VR market hasn't exactly taken the world by storm since its reintroduction in

2015, Zuckerberg has already indicated that he pictures virtual reality to be something that people use to socialize with each other like never before. In fact, the Oculus group is already working on a wide variety of ways to help make socializing in a virtual space feel more realistic by using high-tech cameras to study the body language of an individual who is moving through a virtual space.

Facebook Shop:

While you may not see people using Facebook to purchase items much now, the Facebook shop button is anticipated to see a widespread rollout in early 2019 so it will likely become far more common in the coming months. As the name implies, this addition to the Facebook business page tab will allow users to sell a wide variety of items directly from the page which promises to make directing traffic to your wares a more straightforward experience than ever before.

This makes it even more important to have a good idea of not only what your homepage looks like but your collection page as well. Finding one instance of missing pictures or placeholder text is enough to ruin the brand message you are working so hard to cultivate. What's worse, you run the risk of missing out on potentially viable SEO optimization options.

It is also possible to integrate your Facebook shop with a variety of existing online stores including BigCommerce, WooCommerce, Magento and Shopify.

Ads are still important: While not as much of a sure thing as they once were, traditional Facebook ads are sure to continue to be viable as long as a large portion of the planet's population continues to use the site on a daily basis. This is useful for a variety of reasons, starting with the fact that it allows you to target specific products which, in turn, allow you to determine which types of ads are the most important for your target audience. Additionally, this will ensure that if a customer sees a specific product that they like they will be able to click on it and be taken to that item specifically.

Chapter 3: The Future of Instagram

2018 was a banner year for Instagram with more marketers turning to the service than ever before. While this influx of interest has brought new lifeblood to the service, it has also seen some new changes which means you will need to be aware of the latest and greatest if you want to continue to see results. The following list of trends is sure to shape the future of Instagram marketing in 2019.

Vertical Video:

If you are still looking for proof that all trends reverse if given enough time, look no further than the reemergence of vertical video. While this was once a clear sign that the person who took the video didn't quite know what they were doing, it is now a burgeoning Instagram trend that is sure only to continue blowing up in the coming year. Vertical video is also becoming more acceptable on other sites including Vimeo and YouTube. All this makes it clear that vertical video is not going away which means now is the time to learn to create and edit them properly in order to ensure that you are ready to capitalize on this trend for as long as possible.

If you haven't yet, then now is the time to learn basic video editing skills, even if you commonly work with a video team as it is always a good idea to understand how to edit down a longer video for an Instagram story. To add extra production value to your Instagram stories consider secondary apps like Storeo or Inshot. There are a few choices when it comes to creating an acceptable vertical video, and you can actually trim down video shot horizontally so it looks as though you were savvy enough to hop on this latest retro trend.

It is important to keep in mind, however, that there is a big difference between natively filming in vertical mode and cropping things later and simply hoping it all works out in the end. The most important aspects of the shot that you need to plan for when it comes to vertical video is that everyone remains clearly recognizable which means not cutting off the heads of anyone in the shot and ensuring that you don't end up cutting out any of the good stuff in the process. Current trends suggest that many people feel as though this type of content is actually more engaging than the alternative which means your marketing efforts will see more views and people will consume longer chunks of the content as a whole.

While shooting proper vertical video is relatively straightforward, editing it can be more difficult than you might expect. If you have already edited video then it is certainly within your wheelhouse, it will just take some practice in order to get things down pat. There are a few ways to go about doing so, starting with editing the content on your phone directly.

If you are using an iPhone, then you won't be able to edit vertical video in iMovie which means you will need to go with a third-party app such as Bolt or InShot which will allow you to create vertical videos that still display in 16:9. If you have some more time or want to do something extra special with your video, then you may want to switch to using iMovie on your laptop or computer instead. This is a must if you are interested in adding various layers to your video or things like graphics or text. Doing so will require you to rotate your video clips after editing and then flip them in QuickTime after they have been exported, but these steps are easy to manage after the first few tries.

Even still, if you are planning on creating a lot of intricate video content, then you are likely better off taking the plunge and going the professional software route with something like Adobe Premiere Pro. While this tier of software requires a fair bit of tutorial before it can be used easily, the end result will be superior every single time.

Instagram stories with AR Filters:

A major theme of the 2018 F8 Facebook conference was how augmented reality and virtual reality are going to be influencing social media sooner than the public might expect and one such way in which they are future-proofing their services is by offering more and more augmented reality filters as time goes by. Getting in on these options and becoming comfortable with them as soon as possible is sure to pay dividends in the future.

Not only are the face filters that Instagram offers a forward-thinking example of how AR can be used in traditional scenarios, brands, influencers and creators of all types can also create their very own unique variations on these options through the use of Facebook's AR studio. While only a few major brands like Kylie Jenner and Rihanna have used this option so far, you can expect to see more and more similar entities taking advantage of this option in the years to come. What makes these filters so useful from a social media perspective is that they are only available to those who follow the women on Instagram, which means it not only ensures their current fans feel special, it also gives those on the fence a reason to join up that is advertised, for free, every time an existing follower uses the filter.

Many filters often give viewers the opportunity to try out a filter that their friends are using which means that AR Filters on Instagram stories are literally created to go viral right from the very start so expect to see a lot of growth in this area in the next year.

Offline events:

As surprising as it might sound, 2019 may very well see the return of the physical meetup thanks to an emerging trend of Instagram taking key influencers on vacation to specific locations. While this is certainly an expensive option, it is certainly a guaranteed way to generate a large number of likes and to sell a large number of products in the process. Companies like Boohoo, Benefit and Revolve are already seeing results taking a small group of highly curated influencers on vacation to take advantage of their existing followings. What they are doing is essentially forcing the illusion of the "cool" lifestyle by inviting viewers to follow along every step of the way and buy all of the cool things they see. Outside of this new example of influencer marketing, another new trend that is really starting to take off is curated museums of the "perfect" Instagram picture.

The real future, however, lies with brands like Refinery 29 Rooms which blend real-world exhibitions with curated experiences, giving participants plenty of opportunities to interact with the brand in a positive way and also post about it in a way that is sure to get plenty of likes on social media. While creating an offline experience can be a lot of work, it can be an excellent way to gain lots of followers quickly while also generating sales at the same time. It is essentially word of mouth for the modern age. When a customer has a positive experience that is also worthy of an Instagram post then it is far more likely to end up on their page where all of their friends can see and interact with it themselves.

The cocktail bar Her Majesty's Pleasure in Toronto is a perfect example of a business that took this idea to heart. While boasting a reasonable amount of business most of the time, by simply updating their theme and décor to more directly appeal to women between the ages of 25 and 34, they managed to grow their followers by more than 26,000 a serious accomplishment for a small local bar. The beauty of this approach is that you don't need an existing physical location in order to create Instagram experiences, you can simply team up with existing likeminded businesses and ensure that everyone benefits from the added exposure.

Instagram shopping:

Throughout 2018 Instagram has been releasing and retooling its shopping features, but they are stable enough now that you can expect to see serious traction in this area in 2019 and beyond. Beyond simply tagging products in specific posts, users now have the abilities to tag stories to specific products thanks to the new shopping tab that can be found on the Explore page. Rumor has it that soon brands will be able to link up with influencers directly from within the app and that these influencers will be able to tag specific brands as well as products in their posts.

There are a variety of different ways to make sales from Instagram, each of which will ultimately work better with some segments of the market than others. What works for your target audience may surprise you which is why it is best to try as many different approaches as possible as you never know when you will land on a gold mine. Getting started now will allow you to head into 2019 with a new and improved strategy ready to go.

Ads in Instagram Stories:

As popular as they have become, it was only a matter of time before Story specific ads started popping up and 2019 will be the year that they explode in a big way. Current estimates suggest that around 400 million people watch Instagram Stories each and every day which is ideal because it currently offers a far greater return on investment than a similar Facebook ad due to the reduced costs and comparable reach in some scenarios.

As this is still a young form of advertising, it is important to take as full advantage of it as you can before the price increases to accurately reflect its usefulness. This is the perfect time to try out a variety of different formats for your ads to ensure that your game is on point by the time even more people start paying attention. Rather than cropping an existing photo or creating something entirely new, when it comes to ads for specific stories you can still get away with just adding a top and bottom banner in relevant colors. Taking the time to include mentions, emojis, and texts in the ads will help them look more natural as well.

When considering these types of ads, it is important to keep in mind that when people tune in to Instagram Stories they expect to see casual content as opposed to things that are more highly produced which means you will want your ad to have the same aesthetic in order to ensure that people don't immediately swipe past it. Keywords here should be organic and filter-less videos.

Chapter 4: The Future of LinkedIn

As with the other legacy social media platforms, the next frontier that LinkedIn is going to explore is going to be video. This is obvious for a number of reasons, starting with the fact that LinkedIn is known to take a majority of its cues from Facebook in the first place. If you need proof of this fact all you need to do is consider how much the latest LinkedIn page resembles the Facebook homepage.

LinkedIn is aware that the future is in video and they are anxious not to be left behind. The site already makes it possible to embed video directly into multiple sections of a profile including both the experience and summary sections for that extra personal touch. Real-time video is next on the list of incoming features along with things like Skype integration to allow you to directly to connect to everyone in your network with seamlessly integrated video.

Additional Types of Engagement:

Another area that LinkedIn has been focusing on in recent months is increasing its baseline level of engagement. It has long been a struggle to get people to check in with the site on the regular when they are not looking for work or looking to update their profile. Instead of having a binary level of engagement, a host of new feature enhancements have gone a long way towards shifting how people see the service and your future endeavors with the platform will need to adjust accordingly. Today's LinkedIn is more than a simple resume; it can be a useful tool when it comes to building a personal brand.

Improved Integration:

Several years ago, LinkedIn purchased an app known as Refresh that is due to be relaunched sometime in 2019. The purpose of this app is to link your calendar to your social media account so that each of your meetings includes details on everyone you know who is going to be there. This is just one of the ways in which LinkedIn is working to integrate itself into day-to-day activities. Similarly, they are working on a tool that will allow one person to deliver webinars to an audience that can be spread out around the world.

Decreased Base Access:

In a move to push users towards paying for a premium experience, LinkedIn has been in the habit of removing features from the free version of the site. They will likely continue this trend while also looking to create even more types of accounts with the ultimate goal of getting people besides the standard roster of recruiters, salespeople and the like to start paying for a service they have been using for free for the better part of a decade. The platform's plan for the future can be seen in its implementation of LinkedIn Learning which is a free service to premium members that helps the brain stay in shape and offers high quality education on a wide variety of topics. This all indicates that the future of LinkedIn will almost certainly involve a price tag.

While LinkedIn is likely to continue to change in an effort to remain relevant, it is important to do what you can in order to retain as much of your content as possible. For starters, it is important to back up all of your LinkedIn content somewhere outside of the LinkedIn service. You will also want to get in the habit of doing so every time you make significant changes to your content. You will want to do the same thing with all of your connections as your LinkedIn social network is a valuable asset. Moving these things off-site will ensure that you are always able to get to the data you need without issue.

Marketing Strategies for LinkedIn:

Millions of professionals use LinkedIn in some fashion every single day which makes it a natural choice for a wide variety of marketing opportunities. From building brand awareness to building new connections, generating leads and marketing product LinkedIn can be a valuable tool in your social media marketing strategy.

The biggest difference between LinkedIn and other social media platforms is that it is the only platform where standard marketing practices are forced upon users at all times. In fact, it certainly requires a softer touch overall as the hard sell is considered rude and is generally frowned upon. As this network has a very different audience than the rest, it requires a far more specialized approach if you hope to see results in both the short and the long-term.

More Finely Targeted Connections: Marketers are able to specifically target their preferred audience more easily on LinkedIn than with any other social network. Marketers have access to the exact job role, company size or industry that they know typically buys their product which means lead acquisition is essentially a non-issue.

Remain on the Brain: Thanks to the way the network operates, marketers who have made contact with a potential lead once can easily remain in general contact until the time comes that the client is interested in making a deal. Likewise, if anything changes on the marketer's end, a simple message on the social media site is a low-stress way to reach out and let the potential lead know that the situation has changed. Potential leads will also be able to easily check in for themselves and see what's what thanks to the ease with which status posts can be created and read.

Improve Secondary Types of Marketing: While it may seem surprising, email marketing continues to remain a relevant marketing force as the business world gets ready to move into the third decade of the twenty-first century. Once you are already connected with a potential customer on LinkedIn, it then becomes much easier to write a letter that appears to be personalized that invites them to join your email newsletter. You can only message 50 people at a time, but your success rate will likely be a minimum of 50 percent. Just be sure not to abuse this strategy, one unsolicited request to join a newsletter is likely fine, a dozen, not so much.

When writing this invitation, it is important that you make it as clear as possible just what the reader is going to be getting out of the bargain. While they will be gaining valuable knowledge, unless you are known for giving talks or seminars, what you have to say is likely not enough so don't be afraid to offer a value-add as well.

Sponsored Updates: Sponsored updates are likely something that you will want to look into as well. This method will allow you to pay to include a specific post in the newsfeed of a set number of individuals. The biggest difference between LinkedIn and other social media platforms in this instance is that you can target a far more specific segment of the audience including things like groups, schools, skills, job function, job title, company name and more. This will make it much easier to reach your target audience without having to fight against the noise from irrelevant alternatives.

This type of update can also be an outstanding way to promote the type of content that can make you a thought leader in your chosen niche. It is important that any advertising of this type feels extremely well-thought out and includes a call to action as part of the bigger picture. This is because people are tired of traditional adds and will almost always skip past them if they don't feel as though there is anything unique or interesting to see right from the start. Those who are likely to view your content won't sit through something that is purely advertising content. They expect something useful out of the experience as well. By promoting content via a LinkedIn Sponsored Update, a specific firm can target those that will benefit the most from the content in question, generating additional leads as a result.

Quality content is key: When creating this type of marketing content, it is important that the end results accomplish two primary goals: The first of these is that it should provide your target audience with something that will make their jobs easier or solve a common problem. Second, it should do something to establish you as an authority in the space. When reached, each of these goals will naturally lead to more business, it might sound simple, but it is the most straightforward path to seeing the results you are looking for.

What's more, meeting your goals will go a long way towards putting you on track to gain the type of momentum that causes LinkedIn to put their own spotlight on your brand. They often feature or curate trending content by highlighting it in one of their categories. This is an easy way to gain a minimum of tens of thousands of new eyes which means it is an effective way to improve visibility that can't be duplicated elsewhere.

Another way to promote this possibility is to join as many relevant groups as possible and do what you can to stay active within them once you join. This will not only make it more likely that a larger number of targeted individuals will see the content that you create, but it will also make it easier for you to get the inside scoop about what your target audience thinks about relevant issues. As an added bonus, you can message anyone who shares a group with you directly, even if you aren't connected which makes it a great way to build relationships with new possible clients.

If you can't find a group that fits your target audience to a tee, then there is no reason not to take things a step further and create your own. Once you do so, you can populate it by going out and joining groups that your target audience is likely to be a member of. Once you have been given member status, you can filter out the undesirables and then send personalized invitations to the rest with a valid reason why the group should exist. Not only does this new group feature nothing but potential prospects for whatever you are marketing, you are the moderator for the group so you can ensure that no other likeminded individuals come along and steal your thunder.

Not only is this new group a great place for you to show your own expertise and generate perceived value, but your approaches also won't feel like spam because they opted into the group. You will also have a natural built-in focus group, email list, core prospects, the list goes on and on.

Ensure the company page is relevant: You should also take the time to ensure that your company page is regularly updated to provide a consistent and concise message for your brand at all times. This means that the content, colors, and imagery need to all be on point and in line with anything that your website and other social media profiles as well. You will want to ensure that this page is regularly updated to ensure that your brand appears busy and making plans for the future. It is important to only utilize a company page if you plan on updating it regularly because having an outdated company page is worse than having none at all. Having an outdated page shows that your brand is out of touch and can't be bothered to interact with people on this particular social media site.

Along similar lines, it is important to use your custom URL for your business page as it indicates your overall level of professionalism and dedication to your clients, particularly those who are in the B2B sector or professional services. This is important because researching and googling new potential acquaintances has become a common practice and having a personalized LinkedIn URL will make it more likely to show up on the first page of search results.

Finally, it is also important to take the time to fill out the most commonly ignored section of a LinkedIn profile: the summary section. This section provides you with a full 2,000 characters to speak to your target audience in a persuasive, direct fashion. You aren't given a large number of opportunities to use the hard sell when it comes to LinkedIn, and this is one of them. It is important to use this opportunity to address the pain points you aim to resolve for your target audience, while also introducing yourself as a person to give your profile that personal touch. This is also a great place to include your contact information, regardless of wherever else it appears on your profile as this information cannot be overstated; the easier it is for others to reach you, the better.

Chapter 5: The Future of Twitter

Researchers from MIT released a study in early 2018 which looked at the ways in which false information was spread throughout the internet. Their primary takeaway is that misinformation is likely to spread about six times as quickly as true information. From a marketing perspective, this can make it easy to wonder if there is enough fake information already floating around on Twitter to make the possibility of getting any new information out there extremely difficult.

Luckily, it will still remain possible to make a profit from Twitter, as long as you keep the following tips in mind. Before deploying a new strategy, it is important to understand the current state of Twitter to avoid making common mistakes while you still have time to pivot your primary strategy. Twitter is without a doubt one of the most commonly used platforms by advertisers looking to get the word out about their products or services.

Unfortunately, Twitter has been dealing with a number of issues lately that need to be dealt with effectively in order to ensure the process is as effective as possible. Perhaps the biggest issue at the moment is the bots which have taken over in an aggressive way. In fact, about 15 percent of all of the users on Twitter are currently bots. These bots automatically tweet or respond to individuals who use specific words or phrases in their own tweets. While a well-designed bot can be a boon to your brand, using one that is even a little off the mark is going to cause issues these days as so many people are aggressively fed up with them that even the hint of one is enough to make them swear off your brand completely.

As Twitter is hardly the leader when it comes to monthly users, the fact that 15 percent of its registered users are actually bots cuts down on the number of potential people you will reach with any marketing content which is why it is important to adjust your marketing projections accordingly. Bots also make it difficult for a real message to get through as they commonly carry links that claim to go in one direction while in reality sending those who click them someplace far less safe. In fact, studies show that about 60 percent of all the links tweeted out on a given day are done automatically as opposed to by human beings.

While Twitter is making an effort to crack down on bots, many people remain skeptical that this will ultimately end up doing much good in the long run as there is so much false information being regularly spread on the platform. This is because while it may well be possible to stop bots from spreading false news on the platform, stopping real people from doing the same thing is much more difficult.

Thus, the Twitter marketing strategy of the future will need to look for ways to counteract the spread of bots, the middling user growth and the deliberate spreading of false information by real people. While it may be difficult, like any strategy, it can be used successfully if you take the time to focus on ways to play to its strengths while minimizing its weaknesses.

Be more direct:

With two-way Twitter communication becoming more and more common, it is becoming an increasingly normal thing for a potential customer to tweet at even a mid-sized brand with a question that isn't readily available on their site and expect a response. While it might seem like a waste to answer individual questions in this way the truth is it is actually a great way to invest in the long-term growth of your business.

The fact of the matter is that sometimes individual customers need some extra attention and giving it to them could really help transform them into true supporters of your brand. If you do this regularly enough, then you are likely to develop a reputation as a brand that really cares about its customers which is one of Twitter's greatest strengths. In fact, 85 percent of Twitter users believe that it is important for a brand to provide customer service on Twitter.

Being responsive on Twitter adds a level of transparency to a given brand that helps it seem more approachable and helpful, and this trend is only going to continue into the future. A great example of why this case is Dove, which increased its overall market sentiment score by nearly five percent in just three months by doing nothing more than taking a more active response to potential customers on Twitter.

While the right type of service to provide on Twitter is going to vary by company, there are a variety of strategies you can try in order to generate a better response. For starters, it is important to always request a DM when sensitive information needs to be discussed. Depending on the types of questions that you find your brand being asked, this is one of the few scenarios where a bot can be used without drawing ire. A good example of this is Patron Tequila which offers up a bartender bot that offers up cocktail recommendations based on the provided information. While this might sound silly, it increased the click-through rate of specific tweets to their website by more than 40 percent.

When the truly personal touch is required, however, it is important to start by gathering as much useful information as possible as a means of fully understanding the situation. This may include information the user provides directly or, through the use of a chatbot behind the scenes. You could set up a hashtag for things like orders that will be completed accordingly. Depending on the size of your brand it may even end up making sense to create a secondary Twitter handle that is responsible exclusively for dealing with these types of customer service issues.

Private messages are another increasingly popular means of resolving issues on the platform, and the link for doing so is included directly on every tweet. It is important to ensure your account is set up to accept these types of messages, however, as this is not always the case. This can be confirmed by going to the Settings tab and selecting the options for Safety and Privacy and checking the box to receive direct messages from anyone. With this done you can now add a URL with your own Twitter ID into any tweet to ensure the send private message button appears, letting your users know they can send you private messages. You can create your own private message link by filling in your Twitter ID in the following URL.

Create video content:

As with every other social media platform, if you want to see a greater level of engagement in the future, then you need to take the time to create more video content. While sharing videos on Twitter is hardly a new idea, Twitter is always working on creating new ways that videos can be generated and shared with a Snapchat sharing tool on the way as well. If you don't decide to create video content, then you are likely going to be at a disadvantage because by the end of 2019 video views on Twitter are anticipated to grow more than 200 percent.

The reason for this is the perception that video is more likely to cut through the host of false content generated expressly for the platform. Videos are harder to fake which is why they perform better and reach more people when compared to GIFs, images and links. What's more, video on Twitter is actually more effective than video on Facebook at the moment, with the former outperforming the latter by nearly 40 percent.

One of the ways that Twitter users are going to judge the quality of these videos is by the number of views each has received. While this is hardly a true verification of authenticity, it is enough to provide users with a general idea of how many people think the video is worth the effort to watch as well as how far it has spread which makes it easier to determine if its source is likely legitimate.

In order to rack up as many views as possible, it is important to understand what Twitter counts as a view. In this case, a view is racked up after two seconds of playtime as long as the video is taking up at least half of the available screen. These standards aren't high, clearly, so it is important to make a big splash early with your content and go from there.

For starters, this means you are going to want to keep things short and sweet with about 45 seconds being considered the ideal length. It is also important to ensure you regularly use content pillars which are the core types of content that your brand creates and that your videos fit in with the overall theme you are working to create. Common pillars on Twitter include both inspiration and education.

Videos will begin to play as users scroll over them, the first three or four seconds are going to be the most important overall. What's even better, for those who are using video content regularly, Twitter recently introduced the Video Website Card to make videos that are posted as effective as possible. Essentially, the Video Website Card looks like a normal post until it is clicked on which then causes it to open up in full-screen mode with a copy of the relevant tweet beneath it.

The post then also includes a tag at the bottom of the video along with a header and a link to the website in question. When the user clicks on the video again, it then plays in full-screen and they are provided with a new experience as well. This can include things like having a landing page appear or opening the website directly.

Forming connections:

While Twitter has always been about forging new connections between users of all shapes and sizes, this becomes more and more difficult as time goes on. This trend is only going to continue as the future unfolds thanks to two main issues: verified accounts and bots. When it comes to bots, the issue is endemic in a system where the value of a given user is represented by the number of followers that person has. Is it any wonder, then, that public figures of all shapes and sizes have stooped to using bots to increase their presumed reach and thus improve their actual reach in the process?

As there is already an entire industry devoted to buying and selling followers it can be difficult to determine a clear course of action moving forward. A good place to start is with TwitterAudit which is a free service that anyone can use to see an overall quality score for a given Twitter handle as well as a verdict as to whether or not the account is real or fake. Another good way to determine the quality of a given account is to look closely at the number and frequency of their tweets.

According to user data logs, the average number of tweets is less than 72 with that number making an account appear as though it may be a bot. If the account hits 144 tweets per day then in most cases the account is being filled by a bot. Twitter bots are created specifically to influence user perception and behavior which is why it is so important that your brand comes off as authentic, engaging, trustworthy and, above all else, human.

The other issue to consider is the kerfuffle surrounding verification. Originally, the goal of the blue checkmark was to show others that a public figure's account had been verified in the interest of letting the public know the account was authentic. While this process is theoretically still in place, it was suspended in 2017, and an improvement or replacement process has yet to be implemented. Verification was meant to be an easy way to verify a voice and identity but it has since become something else, and this needs to change if it is going to have any real validity moving forward.

The program is likely going to be changing to a more open verification process which could help combat misinformation across the platform. If accounts, as opposed to just celebrities and influencers, could be verified it would give users of all types more confidence to interact with all sort of entities, confident that they were not simply communicating with a bot.

Expansion plans:

Once you have verified that your target accounts are real people, the next step is to find them using Twitter's advanced search functionality. This process can be a little touch and go, but there are a number of things you can do to make it as straightforward as possible.

For starters, you are going to want to pay attention to the difference between the word any and the word all as it is sure to come in handy. Generally speaking, using all will limit the search results while any can be used to bring in more results if your initial search comes up short. When it comes to looking for people, if you know who you are looking for but require a specific tweet to source then you can enter their handle as well as the relevant keyword to improve your odds of success.

You may find some use in searching for places as well,

especially if you are marketing for a local business and want to see what people are saying about the community you are located in. If you are looking to see what people had to say over a specific period of time, then you can use the Dates search which is ideal for seeing the response to an event that already occurred or to the release of a new product. The results to these searches always default to the Top replies, but you can also use the People or Latest option to get the true thoughts and feelings of the masses on the topic in question.

Sharing in Real Time:

Twitter has always been at its most effective when it is breaking news in the moment, and this still remains true regardless of the influx of misinformation it has experienced in the past few years. This is due to the fact that the barrier to entry remains so low that there are still an active group of users continuing to generate content. Likewise, it is extremely easy for a person to retweet something and thus feel as though they are a part of the conversation as well. Due to the character limit, the stories are always easy to understand and straight to the point which is perfect for stories that people only vaguely care about. As users can see how popular a tweet is in real time this issue is only magnified.

One hotly debated trend on Twitter that is sure to continue into the future is how long the ideal tweet should be. To the surprise of many, it appears that longer tweets actually lead to an overall increased level of engagement from followers. The reason for this has to do with simple storytelling as longer tweets typically mean more engaging content. The new thread feature also allows for an even more narrative approach which is why this trend is likely to continue for the foreseeable future.

Threads are especially useful for events that include a series of updates, a multi-step tutorial or long-form interviews; they allow brands to branch out and create types of content that have literally never been seen on Twitter before.

Where It's Going:

The earliest versions of Twitter were first created in 2006, and the sole purpose was to provide a microblogging platform with a hard cap of 140 characters per entry. The company expanded rapidly at first and filed their IPO in 2013. Since then, Twitter has been evolving in some slow, but hardly subtle, ways. Thes days, Twitter needs to worry about keeping shareholders happy, so it becomes easier than it might otherwise be to predict where the platform is likely going in the next few years.

New Sub-Apps and Tools:

Twitter may create a news application: Love it or hate it, it is difficult to argue that Twitter hasn't changed the way the average news story breaks in 2018. The app is already part of the conversation when it comes to breaking news which is why it would make sense to break that functionality out into its own app, which can then be marketed accordingly. There is serious money to be made if Twitter can find a way to take ownership of this content in a way the original creators approve of because it could then license this content out, much like the Associated Press does with traditional news stories.

Twitter will likely start offering paid tools: It isn't a secret that reaching a group of employees as quickly as possible is something that certain facets of the market would pay for. As Twitter already has the infrastructure to support such an undertaking it could very well expand into this space with a suite of tools with a strong business focus. It is clear that Twitter needs to either expand or narrow its focus in order to reach beyond its current user base of around 300 million individuals as at this point the only real growth is coming from those who previously did not have regular access to a smartphone and focusing on the business segment is as good of place as any to start.

Twitter will likely start requesting for more user information: In order to continue serving up more personalized content, it is very likely that Twitter will soon start to request more and more information from users in hopes of matching them with content they would be interested in viewing. This would obviously be ideal for advertisers as it will allow them to target even more precise segments of the market, improving their metrics all around.

Chapter 6: The Future of YouTube

YouTube is, without a doubt, a major force in the content marketing plans of the day and that is unlikely to change anytime soon. There are currently more than 1.3 billion register users on YouTube, and at least 70 percent of those create content in one fashion or another for the site. Current studies estimate that more than 75 percent of all of the traffic on the internet is video and more than half of all web traffic after 9 pm is video traffic from Netflix and YouTube primarily.

With video playing such an important role in social media marketing of all types, the importance of having a strong online video presence is only going to continue increasing as time goes on. From a marketing standpoint, YouTube is especially useful as it provides content creators with the opportunity to form a real connection with the viewer and to really explain the ins and outs of the product or service that is being provided. When done correctly, the average viewer will not only be a converted customer but a profitable pair of eyes on additional videos as well.

First things first, before you can market new content on YouTube successfully it is important to test webpage marketing on YouTube in an effort to give yourself a leg up on the competition as a means of helping your brand reach the upper limits of its popularity.

Reconsidering Youtube:

If you hope to make it big in the YouTube marketing world moving forward, then it is important to reconsider the way you think about YouTube. When it comes to overall importance, it should be considered a second website which means putting as much time and strategy as you would for your primary site.

It is especially important to pay attention to your channel as it is essentially the homepage that ties any and all of your disparate content together in one easy to parse place. Remember, every video that ends up on your YouTube channel strengths the overall effectiveness of your site, and thus your brand, as every video ultimately points back to the channel page and starts the process all over once again.

Since your YouTube page is now being treated as a secondary website, it is important that the rules of good web design apply to this space as well. After all, the more authoritative your channel is, the higher your site is bound to rank. Keep in mind that your videos must remain on topic if you hope to build authority

Video Content Refresher:

As the basics surrounding what makes an acceptable video are sure to change over time, it is important to make an effort to stay on the pulse of YouTube popularity so that your videos always look and feel fresh. Nothing will throw a new user off of your channel for good than seeing a recently posted video look as though it is a blast from the past in an earnest way. For starters, it is important to have clear goals as to what you hope to gain from your YouTube videos.

Viable goals include things like growing the overall viewership of your page or site. Video is a great way to encourage viewers to look more closely at your main site which is the first step to an effective sale or opt-in for your products or services. Using your video to capture leads is another natural choice as it is a quick and easy way to provide a list of benefits that come along with opting in. It is important to track all of your YouTube leads religiously as these are the individuals that are already in the know when it comes to your products or services and a knowledgeable lead every time. When done correctly, YouTube videos are a great way to improve your brand's visibility, and they can even be used to make direct sales via a call to action.

Sequencing Is Key:

These days viewers are unlikely to give a video 10 seconds before they try something new if it doesn't spark their interest. With so little time to spare it is vital that you sequence your videos correctly right from the start. These days, correct sequencing is all about timing, and the perfect length for a YouTube video nowadays is three minutes in most cases and never longer than 10 minutes no matter what.

The start of your video should include proper branding as well as a proper introduction. The days of low-quality video being acceptable are long past, and the more professional your content appears from the jump, the more likely it is that people will actually watch it. It is also important to introduce yourself and your brand and let the viewers know where they can go to find out more information. It is also recommended to go smoothly from the intro into an explanation of what the viewers will gain by watching the video as quickly as possible. You should state the length of the video, so the viewer is aware if they don't happen to be already.

From there, the bulk of the video should follow through on providing the promised information. Avoid the bait and switch at all costs. Throughout your video, you should do what you can in order to ensure it is as clear and detailed as possible. Finally, as with any good message, you must recap what you have talked about and summarize the key points for the viewer. You will also want to highlight the main areas of your service or product once more and give out the link to your website once again for good measure. It is also important to include a call to action such as encouraging the viewer to make a purchase or to simply subscribe to your channel. Finally, it is important to leave a few extra seconds at the end of your video so that viewers have time to click the link before the next video starts.

Improve Engagement:

Moving forward, YouTube is more likely to be seen as a social networking site as opposed to the simple video site it once was. This means that instead of simply posting content you need to interact with your viewers just as you would on any other social media site. After all, the more likes, viewers, friends and overall engagement you have the higher your videos will rank and the more people who will ultimately see them.

Tips For Creating Captivating Content:

Detailed product reviews: Depending on the goals of your content marketing strategy, reviewing products related to your niche or sub-niche is often one of the best ways to bring in new members of your target audience. A review of a product will naturally slip past the standard defenses that many people put up towards sales pitches while still containing virtually all of the same information of a good pitch without any of the traditional stigma that typically comes along with the process. Remember, a review can help customers avoid wasting their money on a shoddy product while a sales page is considered an especially pushy advertisement.

The easiest way to go about doing product reviews is to focus on a single product or group of products with an exceptionally critical eye. This means you are going to want to single out the various weaknesses of the product or product line as well as focusing on its strengths and what makes it unique. It is important to keep in mind that this type of content needs to come off as unbiased as possible otherwise the illusion will be ruined. This means it is important to intersperse positive reviews with negative ones to allow your target audience to come to the right conclusions about your review integrity. When writing these reviews feel free to include two or three links where the reader can purchase the product if they are so inclined.

Broad strokes reviews: Depending on the type of products that are relevant to your target audience, you may find an in-depth review of products to not only be difficult to write but relatively useless as well. Instead, you may want to focus on brief reviews that typically include just a single picture and a few hundred words outlining the product's bullet points before including an overall rating and links to purchase if relevant. These types of reviews are typically most effective with cheaper products where readers just want a little information before making their purchasing decisions.

What's more, these types of reviews are known to generate higher than average click-throughs as users are more likely to click the link at the end in hopes of finding out more detailed information about the product in question. These posts then often include things like round-ups regarding similar products as well as a ranking system of some sort. This is important as potential conversions are far more likely to read one article on 10 items as opposed to 10 articles each focusing on a single item.

Content that answers questions that exist in your niche: It doesn't matter what niche you occupy or what products or services that you sell, your target audience is going to have questions. These questions can range from specific inquiries about the products or services you sell, ways to make more effective use of the same or even general questions about the niche that you occupy. In fact, nearly 70 percent of all search engine traffic stems from people asking questions.

With this in mind, creating custom content is almost too easy, all you need to do is keep track of the questions that your target audience is asking, and then answer them. Not only will this help to bring in new users who find your content via a basic search, but it also helps to establish you as an authority in the niche right from the start. This, in turn, will help to build trust in your own personal brand which will then make them much more likely to purchase a product or service from you as it will be seen as a transaction that you can trust.

To get started creating this type of content, the first place to look is inward at the products or services that you sell. If you are always receiving the same types of questions then this is a great place to start, otherwise, make like your users and head to Google to determine a good starting place. Start plugging questions related to your niche into the search bar and see what turns up. Remember, the goal here is to stand out from the crowd which means you can stay away from questions that have already been answered. Every time you come across a question that doesn't have a full page of relevant answers take note, you are one article and a bit of search engine optimization from practically guaranteeing yourself a spot on the front page of search results.

Outdo the competition: If you aren't sure what type of custom content to create, then do something similar to what your competition is doing, only better. While you don't want to be known as a copycat, having a great, similar idea is an excellent way to stay in sync with what the market expects, especially if you are just starting out and have not yet developed a personal style.

This means you are going to want to make a list of all of the sites you view as your biggest competition so that you can regularly search their sites for new content. After you get into this habit, you will then need to keep it up. Not only keeping tabs on the competition, but also the target audience's response to the content, can make it easier for you to understand what works best so you don't waste your time early on doing things that aren't going to prove effective in the long run. Once you have the relevant information in mind, you can then work to reverse engineer a version that proves even more effective than the original. This will also make it easier for you to keep up with what your audience is currently up to including changing goals, interests, priorities, and behavior.

It is important to keep in mind the needs of your primary users at all times. If they feel as though their needs aren't being met then they will search to get them satisfied somewhere else instead. This is why one-upping the competition is so important. It will help to keep your fans consuming your content where they belong. You will also need to keep in mind that while you are doing this sort of thing to the competition, they are also doing the same to you. Never be happy resting on your laurels, always be on the lookout for the next big thing.

Chapter 7: Keep an Eye on Vero

Of all the various social media platforms looking to take a seat with the big boys, Vero looks to be the one most likely to break into the mainstream. Its focus is on a more "natural" experience that is light on traditional ads. While it has already been around for a few years, the platform has only started to gain traction relatively recently. The exact reason why 2018 has seen such a large jump isn't exactly clear, though both the issues that Facebook and Instagram have been dealing with are likely partially the reason for the success.

If you look at the timeline of search trend popularity for Vero, you will see that it has been steadily growing for the last year, but the biggest spike came as a result of the data breach that Facebook experienced as this naturally lead people to look to alternatives. Its app has already seen more than 3 million downloads, and it was even briefly in the number one spot on the App Store. As a social media platform is only as useful as the number of friends that a new user can add when they sign up, this initial boost of interest may be the shot in the arm the network needed in order to start seeing larger numbers of new users on a regular basis.

The Vero Difference:

While a surface level look at the Vero app will show you something that is superficially similar to Instagram, Twitter, and Facebook except that instead of algorithms determining who sees what, all you get is a chronological feed. Users can post the standard list of links, videos, and photos and also do things like sharing their location and recommend various types of media for other people to comment and like in turn.

Vero is also the type of site with a public manifesto regarding its goals, which makes it clear what the overall goal of the service is as well as who it is for. It believes that people naturally seek connections, but that doesn't mean the user should be the product. The current social media model forces the companies in question to rely on their users' data in order to turn a profit. While currently free to build up a userbase, Vero will ultimately eschew this model by charging a subscription fee which means their users and their customers are one in the same. In theory, this should eventually lead to an improved user experience when compared to the competition which is something the mainstream user can respond to. While common in most markets, the idea that the platform is the product is a revolutionary one for the social media space.

Another unique facet of the platform is the fact that it does not offer any push notifications, and it also surfaces the amount of time that you spend using the app right from the primary dashboard. While this goes to show how committed to the user-first mindset the company is, it also means that those who choose to market on the platform are going to need to be on the top of their game as Vero users will likely do less mindless scrolling than their counterparts for just this reason

Key Vero Takeaways

It was created due to frustration with the current state of social media: The creators of Vero created this network because they were frustrated with what they considered the pain points of the existing social media infrastructure, starting with the concept of the news feed. Users always preferred the chronological approach to the algorithmic one so that's what they've been given here.

Perhaps the biggest change, however, is the lack of traditional ads. Not only is this sure to be a selling point to many users who are fed up with the advertising creep that has slowly taken over the larger social media options, but it also makes those who use alternative methods of marketing stand out all the more.

There are a wide variety of post options: Posts can be television shows, music, text, video or photos while the app as a whole is geared towards the physical experience which is an ongoing trend that shows even Facebook has too much text for the average user. This ensures that every post you make will automatically populate with at least one picture either from your gallery, automatically scraped from link details online or through your camera directly via the app. Vero also makes it extremely easy to add affiliate links right from any recommendation posts you generate. Clicking on the picture in these cases will automatically take the viewer to the relevant platform to purchase it with a portion of the sale going to Vero as well.

More walls between friends and followers: Vero understands that friends and followers are not the same and gives you the option as to how you want to differentiate between the two. Thus, you will likely only need one Vero account that you can use for both work and business purposes. Vero allows users to classify the people in their social network as either followers, acquaintances, friends or close friends and then gate each post accordingly.

There are also no usernames on Vero so other users will see your first and last name if that is how you choose to create your account. When it comes to your profile picture, you are allowed to use any picture that you like without limitation. When it comes to pictures, in general, you will also be able to automatically add a variety of Instagram-like filters, though these are not required.

Getting around: From the home screen, you will find a variety of icons including notifications, collections, user profiles, chat and search which are all straightforward. To create a new post you will want to hit the "+" button which will take you to the "Create Post" page. This will allow you to choose the type of post you wish to make. You can also create up to three avatars that are then associated with your three primary types of connections, furthering ensuring you won't need to set up multiple accounts in order to truly personalize the experience.

The ground floor: While there are more than 3 million users on Vero at the moment, this is still practically nothing when compared to the 330 million people who use Twitter, the 800 million that use Instagram or the 2.2 billion that use Facebook. Thus, putting a substantial amount of work into the space now, will ensure that your page is a premium destination when people start showing up in droves. This is likely to happen sooner than you might think as new big names are signing up all the time with some of the recent converts including Zack Snyder, Selena Gomez, and Rita Ora. The only place you can currently sign up for Vero is through the Vero app which can be found on both the Android and iOS app store.

Chapter 8: The Future of Social Media Advertising

While the average user may not feel as though much has changed, the fact of the matter is that social media has changed substantially over the past decade and the coming decade promises to only bring about more of the same. What started out as a way for teenagers to interact online has since gone on to consist of several billion dollar platforms that have the level of reach that marketers of previous generations could only dream of.

If you are planning on making it big with social media marketing in the future, it is essential that you take the time to understand where social media is likely heading next and how current trends in this space are helping to shape the next generation of users. Before looking to the future, however, it is essential to consider the current state of things.

Based on the most recent Pew Research data, nearly 90 percent of those over 18 and under 30 use at least one type of social media. This number drops to less than 80 percent for those between 30 and 49 and then drops to about 65 percent for those under 65 and over 49. Finally, those 65 and older still use at least one type of social media regularly about 40 percent of the time. Currently, about 75 percent of those over 18 use Facebook or Instagram every single day. While this data is promising for marketers, it also paints a somewhat Black Mirror future where more and more people are addicted to the online space. As those in the youngest ranges are using these services the most, it is important to understand them in order to find success in the future.

Video Is Key:

According to a recent study, in 2019 it is estimated that video content will have a return on investment that is more than 50 percent better than print or images alone. This percentage is likely to only increase from here as video becomes even more prevalent across all types of media and content. It doesn't matter if the videos are leadership interviews, behind-the-scenes content, product testimonials or explainer videos, the important thing is that users are gaining an affinity towards specific brands that will ultimately translate into buying potential one way or the other.

As a marketer, all this content consumption also provides you with all the data you need to understand which channels your audience is naturally drawn towards. This makes it easier to eventually create content that will successfully serve that section of the audience even more readily. The long-term strategy then becomes creating long-form content and then distributing it across the relevant social media platforms.

GoPro is an excellent example of this strategy. They have essentially convinced their users to do their marketing for them thanks to the immediately recognizable style of their user-generated videos. The company then uploads these videos to its YouTube channel, and its more than six million subscribers are then treated to a wide variety of globetrotting adventures. What's more, their clear emphasis on community also works in their favor and gives them the appearance of putting their customers first.

GoPro continues to prove it is a forward-thinking company because doesn't stop at just one type of social media output either. Instead, it also has a very active Instagram presence that is heavily focused on the consumer experience. They encourage the posting of Instagram Stories that are user-generated from users who used the @GoPro tag. This flood of personalized content is what has led GoPro to become one of the biggest brands in the social media space, and it is indicative of what can be done if you take the time to determine where exactly your videos will play most effectively. In doing so, you will be free to capitalize on not only the current trends in   video but also any that come along in the future as well. Regardless of what specific trends you follow, the end result will be a long-term relationship with the community surrounding your target audience that will reap benefits for years, if not decades, to come.

Short-Form Storytelling:

With so many users making regular and repeat use of Instagram and similar sites single-serving content and the storytelling options it provides become more and more attractive and will only continue to grow in popularity in the future. While innately less appealing to marketers than evergreen content, this new bite-sized form of storytelling is already proving to be a big hit with users and the brands and influencers who are early adopters are also seeing success.

As this type of content only lasts a limited period of time, it is only natural that it will take numerous tries before you determine exactly what works for you. Good examples of this type of content that are already on the market include brands like Away Luggage and Everlane which have both done great jobs of capturing user interest through sophisticated, strategic and above all unique, types of ephemeral storytelling.

Everlane hired a group of millennial filmmakers to make a video in a famous ice cave in Canada as an excuse to prove how warm their new jacket was. Not only was the resulting video interesting for viewers to watch, but it also served as proof at how warm the jacket actually was. While this trend is only going to become more prevalent in the coming years, there are likely already examples of brands or influencers doing something similar in your niche which means that inspiration is likely only a few clicks away.

This will make it easier for you to learn what tactics are most effective when it comes to reaching your audience and also the techniques that will help to ensure that your customers are interacting with as many separate parts of the story as possible. This often includes things like talking with customers directly and interacting with them on their chosen social media platform. Direct communication will not only provide you with a variety of useful types of data, but it will also help you to form the types of relationships that lead to individuals becoming brand advocates because they feel that they aren't promoting a brand, but they are also promoting a community.

Of course, it is important to keep in mind in these instances that the types of storytelling that can take place in these scenarios is going to be different from what is possible on other platforms. First and foremost, the content that displayed is far less curated, and the various integrations of the format have the potential to make it more engaging. Stories are already overtaking primary grid activity when it comes to Instagram which means that if you don't learn how to take advantage of this type of content soon, you will, without a doubt, be left behind.

Influencers on the Rise:

Current estimates put the influencer market at a 10 billion dollar per year industry by 2020. Millennials and Generation Z, two big audience groups that will be discussed in a later chapter, are embracing influencers enthusiastically which means if your future marketing plan doesn't include them in some shape or form then you are missing out on a serious potential advertising avenue. Influencers of all types use a wide variety of kinds of storytelling to get their message across which is why their appeal is so universal; there is literally someone for everybody.

This makes an easy way for brands to reach entire communities that they otherwise couldn't all while only working with a single individual or small group of individuals. When it comes to choosing the influencers you are interested in working with it is important to first have an idea of what type of content creation you are interested in focusing on and then go from there. Choosing knowledgeable influencers will make it possible for you to essentially allow them free reign to do whatever it is that they do best. Influencer trends that are on the rise include Instagram Stores that share a unique, immersive experience, a full-spread Instagram grid discussing particular products and longer-form content in the form of beauty, product or fashion hauls.

Courting Controversy

The recent Nike campaign featuring Colin Kaepernick is only the latest in a line of marketing decisions designed specifically to make waves with consumers. As the issue that Kaepernick so publicly supported is so decidedly controversial, it doesn't matter what side of that particular issue you come down on; it is an undeniably bold move on Nike's part.

Other major instances of major brands courting controversy in recent years include Chick-Fil-A expressing their conservative opinion about gay marriage or the NBA moving a game out of North Carolina to protest a recent state law that made it easier to discriminate against the LBGTQ community. Likewise, Dick's Sporting Goods stopped selling assault rifles, and CVS Pharmacy stopped selling cigarettes, the list goes on and on.

What's interesting about all these examples is how they have bucked the trend that most brands follow of avoiding controversy at all cost. While seeking out the comfortable middle ground makes since when trying to appeal to as wide of a base as possible, going hard on a particular issue in an effort to galvanize support behind the side you favor is increasingly proving to be a viable strategy as well.

First things first, taking a stand shows that your brand stands for something and also stands up for what it believes in. If you are choosing to stand up for an issue you actually have an opinion on then your choice will be easy; otherwise you may want to do some market research first and determine which side is going to generate the greatest potential return in the long run. Choosing a side shows both sides that you are willing to go to bat for your beliefs which generates a net positive amount of good will in the process. There is the potential that it will make everyone consider your brand more trustworthy and loyal.

While this is not to say that you are going to take a stance on every issue that comes your way, it is important to take a stand now and then because otherwise, your brand will gain a reputation as being bland—especially if your niche is naturally adjacent to more than one hot-button issue.

Another useful fact about the marketing strategy of "taking a stand" is that it can be used as a means of reinforcing your authority which is discussed in detail in a later chapter. At the very least it will be a good excuse to show off how much you know about the topic in question and the comings and goings of the newsworthy events that might affect your chosen niche. A good example of this would be staying up to date on recent legal developments that have the potential to change how a relevant industry operates. You would then be able to also create your own content weighing in on the topic and its potential ramifications. As long as the topic is well-researched, it will, at the very least, show that you really know what you are talking about which is something everyone should be able to respect.

Now, unfortunately, there are a few downsides when it comes to taking a stand on a controversial issue as well, the biggest of which is that you are going to lose some business, no matter what. It doesn't matter how minor the issue you chose to take a stand on is, you can guarantee that there are some people out there who are willing to put their money where their mouth is on the issue and abandon your brand regardless of how long they had previously been happy customers.

On the other hand, you will find that a portion of the customers that do stick around are going to feel even more loyal than before. As an example, assume you start with 100 people who are slightly positive on your brand before you choose your issue. Now assuming you don't choose anything extremely divisive then you can expect about 20 of those people to be turned off by your choice, 20 would become even more in favor of your brand and around 60 either wouldn't hear about your choice or wouldn't care if they did. Essentially the process removes those who might fall off your brand at some point anyway while also supercharging a core portion of your audience. Frequently, you will gain new support from people that align with your stance. People who were not loyal to your brand before, may become new faithful customers as a way of throwing their support for a particular stance on an important issue.

After all, controversial topics are controversial specifically because people on both sides believe they are right so passionately that they are unwilling to come to a consensus no matter what. This also means that when anyone researches the topic in question, it is likely that the name of your brand will come up as well, providing you with the potential good press for as long as the issue remains relevant. This means that if you are thinking about implementing this strategy, you will want to choose a topic that is just starting to be talked about to ensure you get as much publicity out of your decision as possible.

Even if the topic you choose to support or oppose doesn't make the mainstream news right away, you will still get some benefit from taking a stand if you post about it on your favorite social media platform as it will virtually guarantee that the space will become a hotbed for discussion on the topic. This will not only serve to make your audience feel more involved, but people on both sides of the issue will feel more invested in the brand as a result.

Choosing the right topic can be tricky, especially if the topic you choose starts off as one thing and then gets co-opted into a cause that you do not believe in. This is why it is important to screen your topics very carefully beforehand to make sure that they aren't going to cross any lines that you don't feel are appropriate. Crossing the wrong line can easily spell death for all but the most resilient brands which is why it is important to be aware of the types of factors that can make it easier to predict these types of issues.

Generally speaking, you are going to want to avoid taking a stand on anything related to a longstanding political debate. For example, making a big show about coming out for or against the death penalty isn't going to move the needle much in either direction except when it comes to the most virulent supporters and defenders on both sides. Instead, you may find that you get far more traction by tackling a local issue like teacher pay or traffic laws.

Another important guideline is to try and ensure that your business has at least some tangential connection to the topic you are supporting. This doesn't have to be something that is specific to your chosen niche, but it should be something you have a personal stake in. For example, in the previous example having a child in the school district would be enough as otherwise, you may not gain as many diehard followers and you end up losing for expressing the opinion.

VR and AR

The biggest paradigm shift on track to come about in this space in regard to marketing is the potential inherent shift from a 2D to a 3D interface. Facebook and other companies are already working on creating virtual spaces that respond directly to the spot the user is looking and allowing users to move about in a three-dimensional space.

Facebook is already a pioneer in the virtual space, and it is perhaps unsurprising that content marketing is already being perfected for their space. They are really starting to leverage their strengths especially improved empathy and presence. As an example, rather than a traditional television commercial a car company could make a virtual experience that lasts a few minutes and accurately create something that mimics what it is like to drive one of their high-end vehicles. Likewise, a company that matches purchases with donations like Tom's Shoes could create a short documentary that is far more effective at tugging at the consumer's heartstrings than if the same video had simply been shown on television.

VR is already proving powerful when it comes to eliciting empathy, reinforcing customer loyalty, funneling in new customers and converting those who are only on the fence. In much the way social media platforms changed communication as a whole, VR and AR also have the potential to reinvent the way content, as a whole, is regularly consumed. As these technologies are being created, at least in part, with marketers in mind, you can expect the final product to involve templates that anyone can drop content into, regardless of design or coding skills.

What makes AR and VR so potentially attractive for many people is its potential to alter even mundane errands like grocery shopping where things can be tracked as users move throughout the store so that brands can offer up specific incentives for purchase in real time. Users are already becoming more and more used to constant tracking in the form of digital assistants and the ever-popular FitBit. It isn't much of a stretch to take things one step further and ensure all that data is getting to the marketers who can put it to good use.

In addition, these innovations will open up ways for an entirely new wave of content creators to make money off of existing content by simply converting it to this new format. For example, when visiting a new city, a traveler might pull up an AR tour that includes things like videos, language translation services, and geotagged pictures to name a few, all of which will be prime candidates for their own form of advertising.

Facebook is also working on a type of VR for interoffice communication known as Facebook at Work. The premise of this system is that it will be a closed loop that is unique to the needs of each enterprise client. As most people already have a Facebook account, it is easy to get everyone up and running with the service as soon as the platform is integrated into the existing enterprise API for things like voice calls, conferencing, presentations and more.

If this service really takes off, it will mean the end of work laptops and workstations completely as everything would rely exclusively on eyewear technology to work from wherever they happen to be. All of their data is then synced to the cloud, and any typing that would need to be done would happen with a VR/AR keyboard overlay or from the help of a digital assistant who will accurately transcribe whatever you dictate. The truth is this space is only now being explored which means the possibilities are endless for marketers who get their first.

Chapter 9: The Future of Government Regulation for Digital Marketing

When it comes to reasons why there should be some type of government regulation over social media, it isn't hard to come up with viable talking points: Facebook's congressional hearings, Russian trolls, terrorism recruitment farms, questionable content targeted expressly at children; the list goes on and on. Changes to the standards that social media is held to are already being suggested in many places around the world which means there is almost certainly going to be some action taken on the topic in the near future.

As social media is very much a venue for self-expression, this leads to a complicated conversation in the United States and elsewhere where free speech is valued above all else. Likewise, while a wide variety of sanctions against Facebook were proposed, very little ended up coming of its hearings which also indicates that the status quo might persist a while longer. All told, for the time being, it seems the old standard is still in effect when people start talking about regulation the things they want to regulate typically involve other people.

Negative Effects of Social Media:

One of the strongest arguments for regulating social media comes in the form of a morality argument claiming that it may be as important as regulating things like of tobacco and alcohol. While this may sound extreme, the argument at play posits the idea that if left unchecked social media will make it much easier for large corporations to control the overall flow of information as long as they can afford to create the right types of content. This will lead to suppression and choking out of those who are supporting positive issues if they do not have the same amount of capital in their war chest to create their own propaganda as well.

While large corporations using the media of the time to crush the opposition in the hearts and minds of the consumer is nothing new, social media also makes it far easier for governments to get in on the action which is only a hair's breadth from a wide variety of oppressive regimes such as what it already appears the governments in Russia and the Philippines are trying to accomplish.

Another lesser-known aspect to consider is how the constant influx of content from social media effects a person's health. The constant stream of notifications and the desire to not miss any new content actually activates many of the same parts of your brain that slot machines use to lure in gamblers, expect in those scenarios someone will eventually win something from the transaction. While this is not inherently damaging to the adult brain, the age at which children start interacting with social media is always decreasing which means this could cause the types of issues that won't be clear for years to come.

The issue is further muddied due the fact that too much regulation can end up oppressing lesser-held but still perfectly valid opinions as it intentionally or unintentionally shuts down conversations that can't happen anywhere else. As there is so much discussion about topics of all types online, it is only natural that a wide variety of diverse opinions would be expressed—expression that might fall by the wayside if too much regulation makes the barrier to entry higher than some people are willing to reach. It is also perfectly possible that the regulation that comes to pass ends up being one-sided and only really helps those in power, further disenfranchising the masses.

It would be difficult to establish who would be qualified to write legislation for social media without limiting future innovation and sacrificing too much of its positive power. Depending on who ends up making and enforcing these rules, the real truth is that they could end up having a wide variety of negative impacts on any side of the issue.

A Curtailed Future:

Another reason to oppose regulation comes from the idea of competition and supply and demand. Too much regulation could also serve to discourage innovation in the space as well. The idea here is that if the current suite of social media services isn't doing the trick, then the best solution may well be to start from scratch with a new batch of services that have learned from the mistakes of the past and created something that solves the old problems from the start. On the other hand, if new entrepreneurs are stifled from the start by nothing but red tape and regulation when it comes to building and growing a new business then why would they even bother.

It is also important to point out that social media under tight control has a working model in the world: For example countries like China who already heavily limit what their people can do and see online. While major online companies out of China like Tencent prove that China can still dominate in this space, it isn't hard to see where the differences in the ethos of the internet come into play.

Personal responsibility is key:

Finally, there are some people that believe that the issue is one that ultimately boils down to personal responsibility. Effective regulation will need to address the idea that people should be accountable when it comes to determining what sources of information they choose to believe. It is not possible to outlaw gullibility, no matter how many problems this might solve. Likewise, the line between providing a space for free speech and one that intentionally makes fraud easier to accomplish is very thin and hard to determine on anything other than a case by case basis.

Finding common ground: While the loudest voices on both sides don't seem all that interested in compromise, there are a few logical paths towards reconciliation that indicate a possible middle ground could hypothetically be reached. After all, there is a difference between ensuring social media isn't actively being used for malicious purposes and thinking that the government should have the final say on what can be posted to social media in the first place, the dystopian future that those on one side of the argument seem to fear. Likewise, those same people don't want to allow those with the most funds to dictate the truth by spreading misinformation and shouting over all the opposition. Thus, in any conversation about regulation common sense at least has an avenue to prevail.

Chapter 10: The Future of Email Marketing

There are a wide variety of trends emerging that point towards the future of email marketing, what follows are those that are likely to be the most important in the years to come.

Ads Matter less, Creativity Matters More:

People Trust ads Less: The days of the average consumer trusting the average advertisement are long past. Decades of being burned by products that turned out to be far less than they were implied to be have created a consumer that is only interested in first-hand accounts from people just like them or content from sources that have done the legwork to be considered truly reputable. This is why more and more money is being diverted into alternative types of marketing, referral partnerships and influencer associations as these are all means that deliver clear value to the consumer. Unless traditional ads start providing this type of value, this trend is only going to become more dominant as time goes on.

More and more attention will be paid to creative approaches: Paradoxically, the most important trend to follow these days may well be aiming to be as unique and creative with your approach as possible. It is important to do your research first and ensure that your approach is likely to resonate with your target audience, but other than that practically anything you can imagine is fair game. It is also important to consider the possibilities inherent in integrated campaigns or by using creative distribution tactics that focus on engaging the audience in little-known or unexpected ways as a means of getting ahead of the competition who is still thinking inside the box.

When it comes to creating unique content that breaks down traditional barriers, it is only natural to break down internal barriers as well. As more and more marketing teams are taking risks and trying new things, those that are forced to deal with the endless red tape endemic in the traditional business world will have no choice but to fall behind.

The fact of the matter is that companies that put up an artificial barrier between departments are only setting themselves up for failure in the long run. The most successful companies are those that are made up of a variety of departments that all flawlessly work together. After all, creating content that is truly engaging doesn't just benefit the marketers, it can lead to lower costs, improved relationships and better talent across the board.

More attention needs to be placed on how the customer communicates: It would be an understatement to say that technology has evolved remarkably in the past decade. By now, the image of a child trying to pinch and zoom a magazine or trying to make a call on an analog watch are commonplace, and most customers tend to act in exactly the same way in that they expect companies to communicate with them. This is why it is so important to understand the communication preferences of your customers so that you don't end up missing out on potential opportunities without even realizing what has occurred.

When it comes to how customers are likely to behave in the future, some analysts believe that about 50 percent of all Google and Bing searches will be made via voice search by 2020. As more and more people come of age in a world run by virtual assistants, it is not hard to picture this type of future coming to pass.

When it comes to automation, these advances are sure to help marketers of all levels scale more easily while also making decisions based a greater breadth of available data which will, in turn, help them save money while at the same time generating superior results. As automation increases, however, it is only natural that the personal connection that used to define many brand relationships begins to decline. As such, it is up to marketers to ensure that they go the extra mile to reintroduce that personal touch. Without a doubt, going the extra mile will always lead to more committed clients that stick around for longer and spend more money as a result.

Focus on Targeting and Segmenting:

When it comes to utilizing an email marketing campaign successfully, segmenting and targeting the correct portion of the population is a vital part of building the types of guaranteed effective marketing strategies that will see results every time. According to a study done by HubSpot, emails that are properly targeted and segmented are 58 percent more likely to lead to some type of conversion. The profit from the emails that are targeted in this way tends to also be about 20 percent higher as well.

As a whole, email marketing is becoming smarter with an increased focus on those who are prone to actually engaging with content as opposed to those who systematically fail to open any provided correspondence. This, in turn, will free up more resources to target the types of consumers who regularly visit your site and interact with your content. Nurturing these types of consumers will ultimately lead to greater levels of engagement, even if it simply starts with additional emails prompting them to take action.

Interactive and text-only emails: While it might seem surprising, there is an increasing trend towards text-only emails which marks a noted shift from the trend of the previous decades. This is due to the fact that numerous studies show that there are so many variables when it comes to viewing images on Smartphones that it is better to use text-only emails that include links to additional relevant content that contains pictures if needed.

While an email newsletter that is filled with pictures might seem more eye-catching in theory, the fact of the matter is that it comes off to many readers as though they are being bombarded with advertisements which come off as spam. Plain text messages also have a more personal feel as it is very rare that a personal email will contain any embedded pictures. This, in turn, makes them feel less sales-oriented overall while also coming across as more personable and sincere.

Another hot trend in types of emails is increased levels of interactivity. As a means of keeping audiences entertained and promoting engagement, many marketers are working to create emails that encourage new engagement via the likes of GIFs, contests, games, surveys, quizzes, etc. The call to action is then nestled in between the interactive bits giving the viewer more of a reason to stick around and continue engaging in the additional content at the same time.

Increased Storytelling:

While using either plain text or interactive content approach is a good start, an increased focus on storytelling is also an emerging email marketing trend that is an effective way of grabbing the attention of viewers and ensuring they remain engaged throughout the email. Ideally, the marketing message would start with the introductory portion of the story before tying it into the overall agenda of the email and returning to it now and then while also highlighting the products and services on display, news, value adds and the like that the viewer consumes without thinking twice about it.

When storytelling is combined with segmenting and targeting it allows you to create the type of target story for each portion of your audience that you can be relatively certain will pull them in and maximize your reach. This makes them an almost guaranteed positive return on investment and one that is worth looking into more closely in the future.

Increased Focus on Mobile:

One of the clearest future trends when it comes to email marketing is an increased focus on mobile-first content. Current statistics already show that more than 50 percent of all emails are already opened first on a mobile device, and this number is only growing. What's more interesting is that of those emails that are first opened on a mobile device is that only about 25 percent are opened again on another device at a later time. The list of stats goes on: Of the over 900 million people who use Gmail as their primary email client, 75 regularly open emails on their phones. What all this means is that the trend is becoming such that, if you don't focus on mobile right out of the gate, you might not get an opportunity to share your message at all.

Increased Privacy:

It doesn't take a futurist to see that the public sentiment on privacy is only growing stronger as time goes on. In fact, outside of the United States, regulations are already changing when it comes to improved policies regarding the privacy of an individual's personal information. This change in policy will continue to affect the ways in which data is gathered and shared. The European Union's General Data Protection Regulation likely just the first drop in a very deep bucket. While this may not directly affect your email marketing policy, it is important to perform your due diligence and make sure there aren't any holes in your current operating procedure that could leave users' personal data at risk.

While the last decade has proven that predicting technology advancement is a tricky business, some trends are so prevalent that ignoring them is practically impossible. The growing trend towards privacy is a fine example of this. It doesn't take a genius to see that communication options that prioritize privacy are going to continue to gain popularity which means that social media marketing in the future will need to take this fact into account in order to continue to be effective.

Increased Personalization:

While viewers are becoming more and more trained to give out as little personal information as possible, at the same time they are growing used to consuming an increasing array of personalized content. Luckily, automation is also improving which means that automated emails are becoming more viable as well. These emails will automatically include each user's name, information unique to their account and then details based on the segment of the audience they fall into. Future trends in this space include the ability to sort contacts by "buying personality" and a wide array of desired behaviors.

The end result is content that has been personalized as thoroughly as possible to ensure that each email feels relevant to their personal thoughts, feelings, and actions. Taking advantage of strategies like these will allow marketers to provide content that feels tailored and personalized without spending all their time crafting bespoke emails.

Artificial Intelligence:

Some companies are already testing the water in the artificial intelligence space by using it to enhance their email marketing strategies and increase their personalization significantly. In fact, AI is already being used to help with a wide variety of email marketing tasks including things like coming up with killer subject lines, automatically locating relevant pictures and determining how likely a given approach is to lead a segment of the user base to open the email in the first place.

Soon this technology should even be able to offer up the odds that a given email approach is going to cause a specific user to unsubscribe from the list. The demand for AI in email marketing is growing so quickly that it is expected to be a multibillion-dollar industry all by itself by 2025 at the latest.

Adobe has recently released its own version of AI technology that offers up a series of extremely complex algorithms created from dated culled from email campaign responses as well as monitored audience behaviors which found that 60 percent of personal emails and 80 percent of work emails will be opened by the average individuals. What's more interesting, however, is that email marketing was one of the most preferred means by which a brand could contact a potential customer. As time goes on, the algorithms that power AI will only become more powerful and the impact they will have on email marketing all that more profound.

Chapter 11: Snapchat:

One of the fastest growing social media sites of 2018 is Snapchat, and it is easy to see why as it is one of the most popular social media sites for millennials and Generation Z alike. Snapchat currently reaches about 50 percent of those in the premium 18 – 34 range which means that if you are targeting this group, then focusing on Snapchat marketing needs to become a priority sooner rather than later.

There are a wide variety of ways to advertise on Snapchat, and while some of these options are priced prohibitively for smaller marketers, the range of options means there should be something for everyone. One of the most popular means of advertising on Snapchat that most people see is the Discover tab which provides quick access to trending stories, event coverage, viral topics and the like from major names and major brands. The cost to be featured here is around $50,000, but it is an easy way to ensure you reach virtually all of the daily users of the app.

The next option is Sponsored Lens which appear when a photo is taken in a specific area. When a user holds their finger on the screen, they will be presented with a variety of different sponsored lens that alters their content in some way. While you might not think about these lenses very much, or use them yourself, the fact is they are big business and cost a minimum of $500,000 per day depending on the location. The reason for the cost is that they cover a wide area and generate tons of impressions as they are almost guaranteed to be seen whether or not they're actually used, and the potential for a specific lens to go viral and become extremely popular in the short-term is relatively high.

Snap ads are a more reasonably priced option that places an ad in between longer features on the Discover tab that automatically play while the user is consuming content. These ads last 10 seconds and provide the user with the option to interact with the ad in order to see additional content. This is an increasingly popular trend on the platform, and these ads are already seeing upwards of five times as many clicks as those on other platforms. When done correctly, a Snap Ad blends in with the other snaps the user is viewing which means by the time it is clear to the consumer that it is an ad, it is likely already over or nearly completed. Snap ads currently cost about $1,000 per ad.

Another new trend for Snapchat is Snap to Unlock Codes which are essentially a variation on the traditional QR code that look like a yellow ghost surrounded by dots. When a user snaps this code, they then gain access to unique filters or other special offers. These codes can then be connected to time-limited deals, specific coupons, and similar deals.

If you are marketing for physical locales or events, then a Local GeoFilter is another emerging trend that allows marketers to create filters that are active within a certain location. The cost for this type of advertising varies based on the size of the location in question and the length of time for which it is active. For example, if you were interested in creating a filter to run during the three days of a marketing conference, active only at the relevant conference center, then the cost would be around $20. These can be set up for any location, venues, neighborhoods, communities, and is a relatively inexpensive way to generate brand discussion and exposure.

Chapter 12: Facebook Messenger Ads

The Facebook messenger app is home to nearly 1.5 billion active users, making it the largest messaging app in the United States and one that is likely to remain viable regardless of how strict privacy concerns become on more traditional social media sites. Currently, around two billion messages are sent through the app each month according to Facebook's own data, and a growing subset of those users are using the app to communicate with businesses directly. In fact, a recent study shows that more than 60 percent of those polled they actually enjoyed getting messages from business and more than 65 percent said they would be fine with receiving more of these types of messages in the future.

Advertising on the Facebook Messenger app comes in several forms, the most straightforward of which runs a sponsored message on the app's home screen. These messages are seen between conversations and are clearly labeled with the word sponsor above the name of the advertiser. If you are unsure how effective this type of advertising might be for your company, there are a number of ways you can test the waters before jumping in with both feet.

For starters, if you have a feeling your customers are likely already using the app, then you would want to include the app in current campaigns using available creative and targeting. Facebook will then automatically do what it can in order to get the best results possible. You will then be able to directly compare results from the

News Feed and results from Messenger in reports side by side.

The next option is to use Click-to-Messenger ads which allow advertisers to run a specialized campaign that asks users to communicate directly via a click-to-Messenger. This makes it possible for consumers to easily ask any questions they might have and even allows the advertiser to provide relative support at the moment as needed. This can be an extremely effective way for brands to show customer's they care and the results speak for themselves as brands with a direct line for question tend to see about 50 percent more conversions on average. The opportunities to communicate directly via the messenger are only going to continue improving as time goes on, making this option an emerging trend to watch moving forward.

Instead of a simple communication option, a call to action button is also an option. A call to action button is similar to a straightforward communication option except that it includes a wider variety of options including things like Shop Now, Sign Up, Subscribe, Watch More, Send Message, Request Time, Learn More, Get Showtimes, Contact Us, Book Now, Apply Now and See Menu. After the conversation is started, the target audience is then provided the predetermined message that you generate at startup.

This then gives businesses the option to interact with each person individually, answering their questions or scheduling appointments via bots or live chat. A great example of this type of service is Sephora who saw a 10 percent increase in successful bookings after implementing a chatbot system.

The next option involves delivering sponsored content directly to active conversations that are taking place within the messenger feed. This is an effective and easy way to provide new details to current users when it comes to things like sales and promotions. Another option allows for the sponsored content to show up within the active conversations feed. This is an effective and, more importantly, simple way of letting existing customers know about relevant sales and promotions. These messages are limited to users who have already connected to your business through the app, however, so groundwork needs to be laid before this option can be effective. Those who will see the most success with this type of advertising are those who already have a fairly large following.

Chatbots:

There are currently around 200,000 bots active in Facebook Messenger with more coming online every day and it is anticipated that this trend is just now picking up steam. Bots can be used in a variety of ways, starting with being programmed to provide specific answers to a handful of questions. More advanced bots are powered via advanced machine learning algorithms and can respond, in real time, to a variety of evolving conversation models. In addition to the data they are initially programmed with, this type of bot can learn from each interaction it has and improve its responses over time.

Messenger Chatbots are already being designed to increase platform functionality in a variety of ways and to help users complete various tasks without exiting their primary communication app. Deciding to utilize chatbots as part of a marketing strategy has numerous different benefits, starting with the fact that it offers up another layer of personalized experience that doesn't feel forced. Chatbots are ideal when it comes to helping to guiding users to specific products, helping them navigate the ins and outs of your site and creating a user experience that is unique for each customer.

They can be configured to run on your site whenever someone visits, or they can be configured so that specific bots run on various pages to improve conversion rates in very specific ways. Everyone knows that marketing doesn't stop at the customer acquisition phase and chatbots are just the ticket when it comes to keeping people engaged. Chatbots are also excellent when it comes to tracking, and even analyzing, customer purchase data. With access to this data, it is then much easier to ensure your campaigns are targeting the right segment of the audience based on the proper behavior patterns.

If that wasn't enough, chatbots can also be programmed to deal with a majority of the customer service inquiries that most businesses come into contact with on a regular basis. If a website has an FAQ section, then it has enough data to create a chatbot that will often send a majority of users away completely satisfied with the experience. Then, if things get too outside the box, the bot can be configured to either seamlessly transfer them to a live person or take the transcript of the conversation and send the whole thing to the relevant customer support person.

Even if using a chatbot in one or more of these functions takes care of 30 percent of the customer emails that typically come in, this is still a significant amount of time that the customer service and marketing teams have to deal with the types of more complicated issues that still require a human touch.

Due to the fact that social media marketing is so common these days, using chatbots to engage with social media followers is another great way to keep users within the app as much as possible. Jumping between apps is still a hassle in many instances which is why offering bots that do it all within the app is so effective and makes the idea of a seamless experience so appealing to many people.

This, in turn, makes it far easier to streamline the marketing process than it might otherwise be. Bots, at varying stages of the process, can serve to funnel users from the market research stage all the way to the acquisition stage and even beyond. Bots can streamline the process of collecting research and survey data by moving each user through the questionnaire at their own speed which means that overall completion rates will increase and the results will also be more accurate as any confusing questions can be easily answered in the moment. These surveys will still end up feeling warmer and more personal than a more straightforward version as the human touch is not only felt but often enough to swing the results.

While they are becoming more versatile every day, chatbots are not yet ready to completely replace humans in all capacities. For the near future, they will be limited to repetitive, predictable, basic tasks that allow the human members of the team to focus more completely on creative work. Likewise, even the best chatbot is not something that can operate on its own indefinitely, it still requires a handler to check in now and then and ensure everything is working properly and that the bot is still bringing in the latest data. Generally speaking, the success a bot sees will likely rely on the various member of your team working together to generate the sort of thing that solves key problems for the customer as easily as possible.

Likewise, chatbots will not replace a full-fledged human customer service department. Chatbots are great when it comes to solving a single issue, but the current versions still tend to fall apart when things get too complex. In fact, generally speaking, the more singularly focused a bot can be, the more effective it will likely be as well. Much like your landing page, it needs to clearly define one issue that it solves for the client and then figure out various ways of helping it reach its goal. Above all else, a good chatbot is flexible which is why it needs to be easy to tweak to account for userbase changes over time.

Overall this type of marketing provides the opportunity for a level of personalized service that is traditionally off the table for smaller brands. It is not immune to poor use, however, which is why the research phase is so important. Otherwise, you will end up with a chatbot that does little but alienate and frustrate customers.

Chapter 13: Tips on Cultivating a Unique Presence

Generally speaking, the word expert and the word authority are used interchangeably, this is not the case with affiliate marketing, however, where being an authority provides you with countless benefits and being an expert counts for little, if anything in the long run. Specifically, in this case, an expert is someone who knows a lot about a certain niche while an authority is the person that all of the experts agree is the first stop for information on a given niche. To put it another way, authorities aren't authorities because they say they are, they are authorities because when they make declarations in regard to their niche of choice, other people listen.

While being known as an expert in your chosen niche or sub-niche is impressive, there are plenty of other experts hanging around, but there can only ever be a small number of authorities (by definition). If you can find yourself in this position, then you can expect plenty of eyes on your website and legions of adoring fans. As such, in this position, you will be able to stop worrying about looking for ways to grow your audience and can rest assured that those in your chosen niche will seek you out instead.

A large part of becoming an authority is ensuring that the level of trust between you and your readers is at the point where they can essentially take everything you say as fact. The most surefire way for someone to build their authority is to always be right, not just sometimes, or even most of the time, but every single time you make a definitive statement. When you finally make it to the point where you have earned the trust of those who visit your site, you will want to hold it as the gold standard of importance and never do anything to make these people think less of you.

Be Mindful of Tone:

While you should already know what type of content your target audience will be expecting, the way in which you present this information is going to be equally vital when it comes to showing them that you are just alike, except for the fact that you know more than they do. To accomplish this task, you are going to want to make an extra effort to get into their minds, speak as they speak, think like they think and use the same references that they use to relate to one another. The easiest way to do so is to consult your demographic data and pick the largest section of it to adopt as your own.

If your target audience is under 30, then the best way to ensure that you are all on the same page is to visit YouTube.com and listen to the current tastemakers on the niche in question. If you have a niche that is focused more on those over 30, then the time you spent studying the niche should be enough to push you in the right direction. Assuming your target audience is younger, then you will want to watch videos made by content creators with the most views as this shows that they are doing something that the target audience really responds to. Understanding the sound of your target audience will make your claim to authority more believable because you will sound like a peer rather than a researcher.

Once you have the language and tone down pat, the next thing you will need to do is to go over the image you are presenting to your target audience with a fine-tooth comb. Additionally, you will want to consider what, aside from being an authority, you are trying to convince your target audience of and what you are trying to get them to do.

Tones to try

• Informal: It is best not to start out with an informal tone right out of the gate as new readers can be put off by what can feel like an unearned familiarity. It is fine to adopt it over time; however, you will need to be careful to ensure you maintain your authority at the same time. The best way to do so is to ensure you remain passionate and enthusiastic about your topic while mixing in more detailed insight with the more relaxed phrasing.

• Promotional: While you will certainly want to promote new products or services as they come online, it is easy to go back to this well far too often if you are not careful which means it is important to be especially cautious about rolling out this type of content early on as you don't want those who stumble across your site to assume it is full of nothing but longer advertisements for your products. Regardless of the content you are creating, it is important to ensure you always maintain your authority throughout by including specific, niche reasons, that make the products or services that you are selling worth your customers' time.

• Formal: This is the tone you are likely going to want to start with when you start creating content for your business blog. While it is certainly appropriate during the early days, you are likely going to want to slip into something at least a little more informal over time because you want your customers to feel as though they are talking to a friend when they interact with your content, not as though they are being lectured at. While this is an easy way to make it sound as though you are an authority figure, it is the type of authority figure that people listen to because they are forced too, not because they want to.

Consider your voice: Every content creator has a unique voice, a "one -of-a-kind" perspective on the world that comes through in their word choice and their phrasing. In an extremely competitive online environment properly honing your tone can be the difference between being an authority and being just another faceless expert. You are what sets your content apart from any other, do everything you can to ensure it is unique and compelling as possible. If you aren't sure what the right voice for you is, consider the following.

The best place to start is by making a list of all the words that you feel other people would use to describe you. You should spend some time on each of these words and consider how you might make each as clear as possible when it comes to showcasing your personality in what you write. From there, you may be able to add in the written equivalent of any unique speech patterns that you have. These can be difficult to pick out for yourself, which means you are likely going to need some outside input for the best results. You can express these types of things including the sentence structure that you use, the way you separate your paragraphs, the length of your sentences and more. It is perfectly alright if you can't come up with much right now, the longer you keep at it, the more unique your writing will naturally become.

If you can't come up with much of a voice early on, it is important to let it develop naturally rather than forcing it. Having a forced voice will only limit your voice from developing naturally, and essentially paint you into a corner as if you change it once people have gotten used to it you will risk losing their trust.

Share What You Are Reading:

Another great way to build up the idea that you are an authority in your field is to share what you have been reading. You are taking all of this time learning about the ins and outs of your portion of your niche, you may as well brag a little as it will only make readers think more of you. Dropping a list of names they have never heard of will help cement the idea that you really know what you are talking about.

Before you share the sources of the information you are iterating upon, it is important to vet them thoroughly to ensure everything is as valid as it first appears. Especially early on, you don't want to accidentally stumble upon a so-called expert that is really a fraud that the community as a whole dismissed years ago. Specifically, this means understanding just who created any and all content you plan on referencing, along with their general level of authority within the niche as a whole.

If you pick a source that is reliable, then you can guarantee that it will be easy to verify, while also helping you to ensure you aren't accidentally opening a well-known can of worms within the niche community. While this will certainly take some work, if doing so ends up saving your burgeoning career as an authority within your niche then it will be well worth it.

Spread the Word:

After you have dutifully created content for several months, you will finally have all the pieces in place to show your niche audience the extent of your authority. To get started, you are going to want to become a regular presence on the most popular forums where people gather to discuss the niche. This means you are going to want to join the forums and regularly join the conversation, answer questions and create posts that other people approve of. Making sure to credit your site with the information each time you do.

During this stage it is important to not pander for any of your products and services at this time, becoming an authority isn't about direct marketing like that, the additional sales are something that happens organically and trying to force it will only delay or stagnate the process. After you start seeing forward momentum and increased traffic from all your hard work, you are going to want to implement the final stage of the plan, which means you are going to want to make sure everything about your site and its content is in tip-top shape before you do.

Once you are ready to really put your best foot forward, the final thing you will want to do is to seek out the websites of other experts in the niche and strike up a conversation. Once you have made nice with the neighbors, the next thing you will do is offer to do them a favor; specifically, you will offer to write them a guest blog. As you will no doubt know by this point, keeping a blog can be a significant strain if you don't stick to a strict plan, which means the other experts will likely gladly take you up on your offer.

This will not only make their lives easier in terms of content creation, but it will also establish you as an authority in the niche to that expert's audience because of your broad reach. Once you have reached out to a new audience, it is important to continue interacting with them in a way that will make them want to subscribe to your own newsletter as opposed to getting their information secondhand. This means creating an active social media presence and maintaining it in the long term. Just like a blog, having an active social media presence that reflects your authoritative status is important to looking professional and having a stale social media pages indicates that you are no longer on the top of your game.

While you can repost content as part of your social media presence, you need to really take advantage of the social aspect of the platform and make as many direct connections as you can make. It is one thing to be the type of authority that puts out decrees from an ivory tower; it is much more effective to be an authority that is seen as being out and amongst the people.

Chapter 14: Get to Know Generation Z

No look towards the future of social media marketing would be complete without looking at who the characteristics of the primary future audience who the primary future audience will be. Generation Z is the up and coming generation that was born somewhere between 1998 and 2016 which means they range in age from 20 to 2 years of age. This means they are primed to take over the workforce in the coming years as they finish college and get to work on defining what the future will look like for them.

Foundational Events:

The two major events of the 00s, the terrorist attacks on September 11 and the Great Recession have both had a significant impact on Generation Z, though unlike the Millennials that came before them they, at best, have a hazy memory of the event and its aftermath. Generally speaking, however, as a generation they have no concept of a time when the United States was not in a perpetual war with the poorly defined concept of global terrorism.

Meanwhile, the Great Recession cast a large shadow over the childhoods of many in Generation Z thanks to the financial stresses it likely put on their parents to varying degrees. Both events have likely left much of the generation with feelings of general unease and insecurity that will likely lead them to make more cautious, frugal choices, at least as they take their first steps out from the safety of their parent's shadows.

How They See Themselves:

Generally speaking, Generation Z self-identifies as being determined, responsible, open-minded, thoughtful, compassionate and loyal. There is some dissonance between how they see themselves and how they see their peers, however, starting with the fact that they see their contemporaries as curious, adventuresome, spontaneous and competitive, all things they do not readily self-identify as.

Another interesting aspect of this generation is that their reading comprehension is off the charts thanks to their native familiarity with digital devices and content of all types. When it comes to religion, perhaps the most surprising thing about Generation Z is that it is shaping up to be the most religious generation in nearly a century with about 41 percent claiming some sort of religion compared to just 18 percent of Millennials, 21 percent of Generation X and 26 percent of Baby Boomers.

This may have something to do with why they appear to be more risk-averse to a number of activities traditionally associated with people their age. A 2013 study found that the oldest members of Generation Z were nearly 20 percent less likely to have tried alcohol than their peers in 1991. Safety concerns appear to be up as well as only about 8 percent never wore a seatbelt in 2013 as opposed to 26 percent of teens in 1991. Generation Z also has lower teen pregnancy rates and higher rates of high school graduation than their Millennial peers with Generation Z being 40 percent less likely to get pregnant in high school, 40 percent less likely to experiment with illegal drugs and 30 percent less likely to fail to graduate from high school at the planned time.

How They Feel About Their Country:

One area where Generation Z is underperforming compared to those that have come before is when it comes to patriotism which likely has strong implications for how they are going to feel about the government for possibly all of their adult lives. They may well be interested in looking into alternatives that they feel do a more accurate job of reflecting their beliefs and feelings on inclusion.

It goes without saying that these findings will have strong implications for marketing of all types. While Generation Z looks to be far less likely to accept pro-American brands than generations past, they are going to naturally be more inclined to be interested in brands that actually do things differently. Research shows that there are three main factors that ultimately influence a generation: technology, societal norms, and age.

Overall, they tend to most closely resemble the millennials—which is hardly surprising—with the exception that they are far less optimistic about their future with nearly 70 percent expressing the opinion that the US is headed in the wrong direction and less than 30 percent claiming they felt the country was on the right track. When asked about how they felt overall, 44 percent said they felt worried, and 21 percent claimed they generally felt scared. Of those polled, only 12 percent came up with the adjective optimistic while at least a quarter of older generations felt this way. What's more interesting, perhaps, is that

71 percent felt their lives were about to get harder.

Always Online:

The biggest shift for Generation Z is the fact that they have literally never known a world without the internet. In terms of content consumption, they are far more likely to stream their content in bite-sized chunks and are far more likely to watch content on their phone than on a television screen. In fact, they tend to avoid most television and movies and rarely consume any live programming that includes scheduled commercial break. As they have never watched traditional broadcast news or read a newspaper they are also far more likely than other generations to fall victim to hoaxes of all types.

When it comes to social media usage, just over 60 percent of millennials admit that social media plays a significant role in their lives, something that only 50 percent of Generation Z agrees with. One place where both generations agree, however, is when it comes to the level of public scrutiny available on social media. Roughly 60 percent of both generations admitted to being concerned with the fact that social media is too public which means their posts could eventually come back to haunt them. Of the two, Generation Z is letting this concern change their behavior with a noticeable trend towards more private social networks such as Snapchat.

Generation Z is also likely to share different types of information online than the generation before them and also to take more steps to protect their private information when appropriate. New trends are emerging that show they are also more likely to passively follow others on social media instead of sharing their own personal details. While they may not be completely happy with it, Generation Z continues to use Facebook as they see it as a vital way of connecting with their peers and friends. Generation Z is also one of the primary age groups that can be seen to actively be joining Twitter, largely because it is not something their parents are using in large numbers.

Snapchat has also gained a large amount of traction with this generation as it is much faster to send messages, pictures, and videos via Snaps, than through more traditional alternatives. Reliability and speed are two of the most important things to this generation which means that social media platforms that promise them are always going to gain popularity. While mobile technology and constant access to the internet are determining characteristics of this generation, they also seem perfectly adept at distinguishing between the online world and the world they inhabit when they are not online.

Generation Z tends to spend its time in some type of private communication with the people they interact with in the real world, while mostly using social media to keep up with what is going on in the world at large and maintaining secondary relationships. As a result of this usage pattern, Generation Z spends more time on their smartphones to the point that relationships first developing online has become standard, if not expected. They do not like the idea of using the anonymity provided by the internet to misrepresent themselves, however, and they don't like the idea of being asked to change to fit some predetermined idea of beauty.

Other Issues:

Those members of Generation Z who are not yet in college

(which is most of them) most commonly have to deal with parents who don't approve of the ease with which their children have access to the unfettered wilderness of the internet. Meanwhile, Generation Z can be expected to chafe at the thought of being controlled in a space that they feel completely at home in as it is essentially their birthright. The experiences they have online and the friendships and other relationships they have there are as real to them as any other.

This online lifestyle is not without its potential drawbacks, however, and Generation Z is already proving to be generally less confident in face to face interactions simply because they have had fewer of them overall in their lifetime than previous generations. In a recent study, 72 percent of Generation Z respondents indicated that they are seriously concerned with the way in which each of their postings will be perceived by their personal social network despite still using social media every day. Meanwhile, 82 percent admitted to not posting something they originally planned to after considering the potential ramifications. Despite these numbers, only about 40 percent claimed to have regrets about an existing post.

While millennials generally do not claim that they view race as a contributing factor to their feelings about a given individual when asked if they currently had friends of a different race then them, only 69 percent of millennials answered in the affirmative. Meanwhile, 81 percent of Generation Z was able to answer this question in the affirmative. When it comes to dating outside their race, however, millennials still have Generation Z beat 45 percent to 35 percent. This disparity might be due to the fact that Generation Z is the most racially diverse generation in American history with 48 percent claiming some percentage of non-Caucasian heritage. This is up approximately 10 percent from the average for millennials.

This general policy of inclusion extends to those of different sexual orientations as well with approximately 8 percent more Generation Z'ers than millennials claiming to currently have friends of a different sexual orientation. This tracks with their ideas towards marriage as well, with a general preference for inclusion shown. Areas, where Generation Z seems to be towing the line, include environmental awareness, universal healthcare, and social security.

Another interesting area where Generation Z has more leeway than previous generations is when it comes to discipline. Less than 50 percent of Generation Z is or was regularly disciplined when they broke the rules at home and only about a quarter went to their parents for help on their homework.

Conclusion

Thanks for making it through to the end of The Future of Social Media Marketing, let's hope it was informative and able to provide you with all of the tools you need to achieve your goals, whatever they may be. Just because you've finished this book doesn't mean there is nothing left to learn on the topic, and expanding your horizons is the only way to find the mastery you seek.

Now that you have reached the end of this book it is time to stop reading and start implementing your very own future-proof social media marketing plan. While you likely have ideas as to how to create or improve your presence across a wide variety of platforms, it is important to work on improving them one at a time instead of all at once. This way you will be able to devote your full resources to ensuring each platform is performance-ready before moving on to the next. After all, the goal is to create a social media marketing plan that will last for years to come; you certainly have the time to do things right.

Putting together the perfect social media marketing plan is no easy feat which means you need to commit to the process fully from the start with each new social media platform you take on. Finishing the job only halfway is not an option in this case as a partially completed social media profile, or one that is not updated frequently will only make your brand look dated and out of touch. This means that instead of trying to use every platform out there, you will find far more success by being selective and only getting started with the ones you know you are going to finish. Taking the long-term view on your social media marketing plan may mean getting started later, but the end results will be far more productive. After all, social media marketing is a marathon, not a sprint, which means that slow and steady wins the race each and every time.

Finally, if you found this book useful in any way, a review on Amazon is always appreciated!

Command the Crowd:

The Art of Crafting an Online Presence and Becoming a Social Media Powerhouse

J. E. Ford

Overview:

2 Hours a Day....

That's how much time the average American spends consuming Social Media.

11 Hours a Day...

That's how much time the Average American Spends consuming some sort of media (listening, watching, reading etc.)

2.3 Billion+...

That's how many users Facebook has to date, and growing every day

500 Million...

That's how many tweets are sent out on Twitter every day

1 Trillion +

That's how many mobile video views on YouTube there are per day.

$16.5 Billion

That's how much was spent on Social Media ads in 2017

Wow...

We are living in an unprecedented age where people have never been more connected, accessible and hungry for content. This is also an age where people have the shortest attention span, the most competition for their attention, and the most options for content and product to consume.

This is the age of most.

Everything's happening online now and the conversations are all taking place through social media. If you're reading this, this means you want to learn how to be an influencer. You want to be an influential voice in that discussion. You want to gain followers, supporters of your brand. You want to become a social media powerhouse.

Many books teach you about branding and what it takes to build a successful brand. Many other books talk about how to leverage social media for your brand and how to make money with social media. This book teaches you how to build a brand through social media. By capitalizing on the marketing and branding genius of the past with the technical and practical know-how of the future, you will learn not only how to build, grow and sustain a successful and unique brand, but more importantly, you'll learn how to build a fanbase, leverage influencers, encourage interaction with and loyalty to your brand. You'll learn what it takes to create a massive following on social media and then what to do with that following once you have it.

In short… you'll learn how to command the crowd.

Introduction:

How many times per day do you check Facebook? How many videos do you start watching that you hadn't even planned to watch? How many times do you click from one thing to the next without consciously realizing what you're doing. How many posts, videos and photos do you like in a day?

People are sharing everything on the different social media sites, from pictures of their children to job postings to world news and more! Everything that is going on in the world around us, whether on a small or large scale, can be found on the numerous social media platforms that we use every day, and there do not seem to be any signs of this slowing down. Every day, social media is growing; new people are creating their first social media account, and others are creating accounts on multiple platforms. The odds of social media becoming a thing of the past are slim to none. Whether we like it or not, social media is here to stay.

With all of this in mind, would it not make sense to use social media in the business world? Nearly everyone - billions of people - have at least one type of social media account up and running. What better place to show the world your brand and the things that you are capable of creating? Each social media platform available provides its own unique way of broadcasting your brand to the millions (or billions) of people in the vast virtual audience. It only makes sense to jump in and use social media for your brand's advantage.

The number of Facebook users in the United States alone has reached more than 214 million earlier this year (reference 1), and that number is only expected to keep growing. For nearly as long as Facebook has existed, people have been sharing business information. With the introduction of ads in 2013, the business side of Facebook has increased steadily, and the same goes for other social media platforms such as Twitter, Instagram, and Pinterest. As a small business, how can you tap into the social media market to benefit your brand?

In the pages that follow, you can learn to use social media platforms to launch and grow your business. You can learn how to thrive on social media and expand your customer base, all while increasing awareness for your brand and fine-tuning your marketing skills. We will start from the foundation, helping you to build a strong brand that fully encapsulates what your business is about and the values at the center of it. Then we will shift our focus from the brand to the audience before helping you to develop a social media presence and use it to enhance your outreach. You will learn how to efficiently use social media to increase your return on investment (ROI) and put money in your business' pocket.

Do you want to get the absolute most out of social media for the sake of your brand? Do you want to build a relationship with your target audience that will lead to greater success for your business? Do you want to get your product or service into the public eye and further the mission of your company? We want to help you get there. Together, we will work through the 9 Chapters that follow. The first part of the book is all about branding. It will teach you how to build your brand (whether personal or business) from the ground up, and then how to find, narrow down, and target your audience. The second part of the book is all about how to build your brand on social media and how to become a social media powerhouse. With a strong brand and a strong following, the sky is the limit for you. So, shall we get started?

Chapter 1: Define Your Brand

We see all sorts of different brands throughout our daily lives in the foods we eat, the products we use, the cars we drive, and more. We all have specific brands that we prefer to use over others, even though the products that fall under those brands are generally pretty similar. What is it that makes us decide which brands to try initially and stick with for the long haul? What makes one brand better than another?

Think of your relationship with your favorite brands that you use regularly - what made you choose those brands to begin with? What was it that first appealed to you before you decided to choose that product or service? Once it earned your favor, what was it that made you come back for more? What makes you loyal to those favorite brands instead of their competitors?

The decisions you make while creating a brand for your business are some of the most lasting and important decisions you will make throughout the lifespan of your company. Your brand is the identity of your business - it is the face, voice, and personality of your products and services, and the impression it leaves on customers will determine your business' overall value within your market and among competing businesses. Therefore, it is crucial to develop a brand that effectively captures the essence of the business and stick with the image you have created for it. Effectively branding your business can make all the difference when it comes to the success of your products and/or services.

The branding process can be exciting, but it also requires patience as a successful brand cannot be created overnight - it takes time, effort, and teamwork. The members of your business and branding team need to share an understanding of the goal in front of you and the work needed to be put in. The process might not always be easy, but the relationship with your customers that will result from your labor will be worth it.

Essential Elements of Brand Definition

So, how do you build a successful and meaningful brand for your business? The first thing you need to do is develop a good understanding of the different aspects of your business so that the brand effectively captures its essence. Why did you start the business? Who are you helping, and with what? What is the ultimate goal your business should aim to achieve? Being able to answer these questions is important for successful business branding.

The "Why" Behind Your Company

It is easy to point out which particular products or services have resulted from which brands - *Apple* created the iPod, *Sony* created the PlayStation, and *McDonald's* created the Big Mac - but it is not quite as easy to identify the reason behind the brand's foundation. One thing that has been proven time and time again in the business industry is that the motivation to make money does not alone lead to long-term success. So, why? Why bother entering into competition with countless other brands and risk falling on your face? Why should customers care more about your business than one that belongs to someone else?

The Golden Circle

The most successful businesses worldwide have an excellent grasp on why they do what they do and follow the "Golden Circle" business concept developed by Simon Sinek (https://startwithwhy.com/). As you can see in the diagram below, there are three tiers to this concept: what, how, and why.

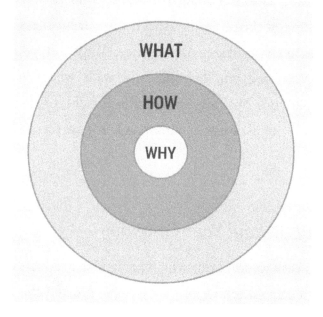

Image courtesy of **tools**hero, Golden Circle by Simon Sinek.
(https://www.toolshero.com/leadership/golden-circle-simon-sinek/)

All businesses know **what** they do - how else could they follow through with what needs to be done? Essentially, every business offers a product and/or service to their target audience. However, the product or service is not the cause for the business to exist, but merely the result of the business' existence. The result of the business is the most visible component to customers, competitors, and everyone else outside the business.

Fewer businesses know **how** they do what they do - they understand the physical processes, of course, but they do not understand what it is that sets them apart from their competitors. How things are done within the business should be what differentiates it from other businesses - otherwise, everyone would be doing the exact same thing in the exact same way, and there would not be a point of having multiple businesses exist. Without understanding how the business functions differently than other similar businesses, maintaining permanent success is not possible. Many people can readily understand what a business does after a very small amount of investigation, but how the business functions isn't as obvious but can still be understood with a bit of effort.

Even fewer businesses know **why** they do what they do - the deeper purpose behind their products and services. These businesses understand that the financial reward is not the primary goal, and the fulfillment of their cause or belief takes the front seat. The "why" behind the business should be at the core of the organization - the foundation for the rest of the business functions to stand on.

The heart of the Golden Circle concept is that the "why" of the business should be more important than the "how" or the "what." Anyone can make a useful product that appeals to the general public - it is the story behind it and the motivation of the creator that sells the product. Your brand requires you to understand and value the "what" and the "how," but a successful brand is driven by the "why."

Your Brand's Mission

The "why" behind your business is exactly what you need to decide on in order to create your brand's mission statement. The mission statement clearly states the purpose of the business, which should be reflected in the voice, message, and personality of the brand. Think about the core values of your business - what is the passion that drives the business? What was your motivation for creating the business in the first place? Crafting a clear and understandable expression of your business' passion is one of the first steps in pushing your brand forward.

Your mission statement will be a useful tool in the future of your business; it motivates your employees and helps them to understand the point of the work they are doing, and it encourages potential customers to trust in the product and/or service you are providing them with. Everything you do within your business should align with your mission statement - you want the consistency to run through your brand so that everything works together properly.

Let's look at *Nike* as an example: the *Nike* swoop is easily recognizable, and their tagline, "Just Do It." is even known by people who do not buy their products. But what is their ultimate goal (or mission)? "To bring inspiration and innovation to every athlete in the world." They do this by creating quality products, carefully selecting famous athletes to endorse their products, and using marketing tactics that enable the viewer to see themselves with those products. The technology they use to inspire and create their products combined with the use of influential athletes from different countries combines innovation and inspiration to reach their target audience. Their mission statement matches the execution methods they use.

So, what do you need to keep in mind while creating your mission statement? Firstly, your business' passion, followed by the demographic of your target audience and the needs they are looking to have fulfilled by your product.

Tell Your Story

Now that you have your mission statement and a good grasp of the "why" behind your business, it is time to tell the rest of your story. Stories bring people together, build relationships, and humanize us. A good story keeps people engaged and holds their attention. Your story should inspire your target audience to commit to your brand and form a connection between you and your customers.

So, how should you put your story together? Think about the person (or people) who have already benefited the most from your business and achieved significant success because of it (every story needs a hero at the center). Emphasize the struggle that existed in the life of your hero before finding your business, and share how their mission aligned with that of your business. The story of your business contains smaller stories within it that can inspire more potential customers to take a chance on your business.

For example, back in 2000, *Subway* launched a new advertising campaign featuring a man named Jared Fogle, the story being that Mr. Fogle lost over 200 pounds by sticking to a diet consisting of *Subway* sandwiches. 200 plus pounds is no small feat for someone to overcome, and *Subway* used this story of success to their benefit by integrating it into their business' story. Mr. Fogle acted as a spokesperson for *Subway* for 15 years, and his success story helped *Subway* to gain a positive reputation for having a healthy alternative to fast food, earning them millions of dollars over the course of his advertising campaigns.

Now is the time to find your story's hero. Dig through your records from the past year and find the customers that have benefited the most from your product and/or service. Of these customers, whose success story are you the proudest of? Find your business' hero and create your story.

Determine Your Audience

Odds are, you had a target audience in mind when you created the idea for your business - if you had an idea for a new type of baby stroller, you probably were not thinking about marketing to senior citizens, right? The strength of your brand will depend on its identifiability with your target audience. To really focus on being a business that your customers can identify with, you will have to create a specific image in your head of the characteristics they have so that you can better understand what will appeal to them. Your target audience will likely expand to different niches as your brand grows and develops new products and/or services, but in the beginning stages, it is best to be as specific as possible about who you are trying to reach.

That being said, determine your target audience - is it, upper-class businessmen? Single parents with young children? Teenage athletes looking for a sports scholarship? What are the typical behaviors of your demographic? What can these people generally be counted on to be interested in, whether out of necessity or personal interest? Every niche has a point of appeal - find your target audience's and use it to your advantage. Knowing how to appeal to your target audience will be useful in attracting and keeping loyal customers. Customize your brand so that it appeals to the specific demographic that you are hoping to attract.

Define What Your Brand Offers

When you are just starting out in your business, you likely do not have a lot of disposable funds. Trying to keep costs low can be frustrating, so try to focus on what you do have. In order to start your business, you had to have a great idea and turn it into something bigger - that is something to be proud of! While you are still in the early stages and are less distracted by the money you will be making, take the time to really pinpoint exactly what your brand offers consumers and make it into a launching pad for your business.

What makes your brand unique? What are you offering that no one else can offer? What sets your product or service apart from the competition in your field? You know who your target audience is, now show them why they should choose your brand instead of a different one.

The Solution for Your Customers

Consider the fact that most customers are looking for a specific product or service to solve a problem that exists in their lives and not just something random to spend their money on. You might be excited about specific features of your product or service, but the end result you should be trying to reach with it is the solution to your customer's problem. What is the specific problem that your brand can solve, and how can you solve it? As you learn more about what your customer is looking for, feel free to enhance what you are offering - what is missing from your product or service that can better help your customer?

More consumers than ever before are doing research on different brands and products before making their purchasing decision, and a positive first impression that stands out above the rest of the brands out there is crucial. Your solution to the customer's problem should be included at the beginning of your story and act as a cornerstone for the identity of your brand.

Better Than Your Competitors

No matter what niche you are in, you should be better than each of your competitors in at least one area - otherwise, your target audience will have no reason to choose you over a different brand. Now is the part of the process where you identify your strengths and weaknesses. This can be done effectively with the help of a SWOT Analysis (using a SWOT template can be useful during this step).

Strengths	Weaknesses
What do you do well? What unique resources can you draw on? What do others see as your strengths?	What could you improve? Where do you have fewer resources than others? What are others likely to see as weaknesses?
Opportunities	Threats
What opportunities are open to you? What trends could you take advantage of? How can you turn your strengths into opportunities?	What threats could harm you? What is your competition doing? What threats do your weaknesses expose you to?

Image courtesy of MindTools, SWOT Analysis worksheet template.
(https://www.mindtools.com/pages/article/newTMC_05.htm)

Analyze the Competition

Part of beating your competitors to make the sale is knowing exactly what you are up against. Do some research and find out who your competitors are, both major and minor, to learn what they do and do not do well. One of the ways you can do this is by creating a spreadsheet where you can effectively compare your competitors to each other and your own brand to see their marketing efforts, quality of products or services they provide, reviews that their customers give them, and more.

After developing a good understanding of what each of your competitors' strengths and weaknesses are, take the time to answer a few questions. Is there consistency within other brands when it comes to marketing and the message they are sending out? How does the quality of competing products and services compare to your own? How does the public seem to feel about what your competitors are offering? What means are your competitors using for marketing that you should be taking advantage of?

Even if you like something specific that one of your competitors is doing, you should never imitate their exact approach - find a way to make it your own. Remember, you want to be different than your competition, and no one wants to be known as a copycat. Innovate the ideas that others have used and make them stand out within your brand.

Identifying Your Idols

Ever since we were young, we had role models that we admired for different reasons (he is good at his job, she is a great athlete, they treat people well, etc.). Likewise, business owners have role models, or idols, that they look to for inspiration when creating their brands. Take some time to think about which brands you admired when you first started your business - what are some things that you borrowed from their methods that have worked well for you? What are some other brands that you should keep an eye on because they tend to have good ideas?

You might even realize that the values of your business were borrowed from one of your idol brands - and that is completely okay! You can have the same values as another company and still be seen as different from it as long as you make the products and services your own. Having the same values as another brand can be beneficial, as you can look to them for guidance on how to implement your shared values within your own brand.

How Your Employees See Your Brand

Not only does a valuable brand positively impact what potential customers will think about your business, but it will influence your employees' perceptions as well. Do they have a firm grasp on the "why" of your business? Do their values align with those of your brand? Do they enjoy the work they are doing or are they just in it for the paycheck? In order to be a successful business, you will want to surround yourself with employees who feel strongly about what goals you are trying to achieve (this can be difficult if the work requires a lot of tedious tasks).

Remember, your employees are the hands and feet of your business - they spend a significant amount of time within its inner workings and can have some very insightful ideas on what your brand should look and sound like. Having a meeting with your employees to get a good understanding of how they see your brand is a great way to figure out what you should keep the same and what needs to change in order to have a good public image.

After having met with your employees and gathered some of their insights on what your brand means to them, look for the consistencies within their answers. What do they all seem to agree on? Does their take on the brand align with what you want it to be?

Finding Your Brand's Voice

Finally, we are getting towards the end of the branding process! This is where all of your work gets put into action, and the voice of your brand is formed. Your brand's voice is essential for proper communication with those you are trying to connect with and sell your product or service to. The tone that you choose to use for your voice is particularly important - it needs to match your brand's identity and the values that you stand for. Your tone also needs to match your target audience - if you are selling gravestones to the bereaved, you should not use a comedic tone, for example. You want your customers to feel comfortable with you and feel good about approaching your brand.

Your brand's identity should remain authentic and consistent; these qualities allow your customers to become comfortable with you and trust your brand, and your employees to better understand the direction you want to take the business in.

Build Your Message

Once you find it, use your voice to let the world know exactly who you are as a business. Let's look at *TOMS Shoes* as an example: one of the first things you see when you enter their website is the message, "Improving lives. With every product you purchase, TOMS will help a person in need. One for One." With these short, simple sentences, *TOMS* effectively lets the customer know what their values are and what they aim to do. Build your brand's message to tell your customers who you are and why they should care about what you do in a simple and easy-to-understand way.

Your logo will be the image that the public will identify with your brand, and it should encapsulate your business in a memorable way. In this step, you will likely benefit from the help of a professional designer to make sure that you end up with a result that you will be pleased with. This is also where you will develop your tagline - a quick phrase that will remind your customers of your brand and stick in their heads.

Integrating Your Brand

The branding process will change as your business grows, but working on your brand will always be relevant as time goes on. Once you have established all of the details of your brand, you should start to integrate it into your outreach methods - if your customer sees, hears, or reads about your business, the brand you have created should be front and center. This means displaying your logo, tagline, and design schemes in your physical location and in your marketing methods (advertisements, business cards, packaging, etc.).

Stick With It

Creating a brand requires commitment; you cannot change your brand shortly after creation unless you have discovered an important flaw. Be consistent with your brand and the representation of your business, including physical aspects, your voice and tone, and the guidelines you have set in place. Inconsistency can be dangerous - nothing will confuse your customers and employees more than inconsistency in your brand.

Advocating Your Brand

Any employees that you hire should advocate your brand as well, so it is important to make sure that they fit within your brand's culture. Customers who have already used your product or service can do great things for building awareness of your brand - happy customers tend to share their experiences with others in their social circles. Allow your customers to leave reviews and share their opinions about your brand on your social media accounts and website so that the word will spread more quickly. Reviews and testimonials can also provide peace-of-mind for anyone who is browsing your site and considering giving your products or services a try.

Advertisements can only do so much to advance your brand. Your brand needs an advocate, and who better to advocate your brand than those who know it the best? **You** and those who understand the heart of your brand need to act as ambassadors, spreading the word about your brand and letting the world know what you have to offer. To get your employees involved, you can hold a meeting or send out a memo to share what you expect of them in regards to brand advocacy, as well as hear their ideas about how to be effective brand advocates.

Beyond Definition

Knowing the finer details about what you want for your brand and how to get there is a vital part of the branding process. As you walk through the necessary steps, be sure to be patient and take your time so that you can be as thorough as possible and not overlook anything by mistake. Consulting with others before you reach the launching stage to gain some outsider insight can be a difficult part of the process, so be sure to take criticism with a positive attitude - do not only choose people who will be honest with you but those who will also present their opinions in a constructive manner.

And with that, you are ready to move forward and focus more closely on your audience and what you need to do to enhance your social media marketing experience!

Chapter 2: Strategies for Your Audience

Your customers are one of the most important parts of your business - they might even be the most important factor of your business. Without customers, your business basically does not exist. Who are your customers, and how can you best reach them? Having a clear understanding of who your target audience is can help you to reach them efficiently and use your resources in the most productive way possible.

In Part 1, we talked about how your product or service should be catered to a specific audience from the beginning and how you probably already had a demographic in mind when you thought of the product or service you wanted to offer. But what if the target audience you should be going after is not as obvious?

Defining Your Target

Narrowing down who your target audience will be is a vital part of any business - you cannot be everything to everyone, nor can you afford to be. Gearing your business towards a specific niche is the best way to start, as you perfect what you are already good at and provide for that niche. You can always expand your target audience after you have established a good following and built up more skills relating to your industry.

Identify Your Customer Base

Who are your current customers? Which demographics are already flocking towards your products or services? Who are the people following you on your social media profiles, who like and share your content and actively engage with what you are putting out there? What do your current customers find appealing about what you are offering them? Which sub-categories within your customer base bring you the most business? Identifying who your current customers are can help you to expand slightly as you look for people who are similar to your customers who might also like what you are producing.

Compare Your Opponents

Take a look at other businesses that are offering something similar to your products or services - who is buying from them? Are they different from your current customer base? If they are, what is it about your competitors' offering that appeals to them? Search the social media accounts of your competitors - what kind of content are they sharing, and how are their followers responding?

It might make sense to go after the same people as your competitors; after all, you want their business. But look beyond those who are buying from your competitors. Which niche are they overlooking that would be a prime target? How can you reach the ones being overlooked with your product or service?

Analyze What You Are Offering

What is it about your products or services that appeals to those who are already buying from you? What are you offering on your social media accounts? Do your followers respond well, or could you use some more engagement on their part?

Think of the different features of your product or service and list the benefits that each of them brings to your customer. Who are the specific people who would enjoy these benefits? You can discover entirely new groups to target by examining your product or service.

Demographics and Psychographics

With all of this information, consider now who you should be targeting as part of your audience. Broaden your search - who can benefit from what you are offering? Who are the people most likely to be interested? Think about age, gender, and occupation, as well as location, income and education levels, ethnic backgrounds, and marital/family status. Each of these demographics holds many different possible audience groups.

Psychographics, as well, should be taken into account when defining your perfect target audience. This includes the internal personal characteristics each person has, such as values, attitude, behaviors, and lifestyle. Think also about personality traits, hobbies, and interests. How would your product or service fit into your target's lifestyle? Which types of media (social or otherwise) do these groups first turn to for information or guidance? Which platforms are most likely to be successful in reaching these targets?

Evaluate your decision

After analyzing all of these different areas, you should feel confident to make a decision about who your ideal target audience should be. Once the decision is made, act on and evaluate it. Ask yourself if your target audience will see the need for what you are offering them and if the price you are asking for it correlates with the demographics. How reachable is your target audience? Your message should be quick to grasp and easy to hold onto, both because of the message itself and the method you are using to convey it.

If you have different niches within your audience - and you should - consider whether or not the same message and method of delivery will work well to each niche. Having different demographics and psychographics within your target audience means reworking your message to accommodate different types of understanding; this is a good thing, as you do not want to set your gaze too narrow and only be able to reach a small number of people. You do not have to do all of the research you need yourself - there are plenty of people who have done this before you, so why not piggyback off of their research to reap the benefits?

Once you know who your target audience is, it becomes much easier to know which methods you should be using to reach them and get your product or service into the public eye. Use the platforms that most appeal to your target, and watch the awareness of your business spread!

Reaching Your Audience

People in the marketing game make it seem so easy to reach out and get new clients. The truth is, it really can be easy - if you know how to get started. Catching people's attention can be done with different social media platforms, such as Facebook, Instagram, Twitter, and the like. However, we are first going to take a look at the one that came before all of these options: email.

Why bother with email when we have all these other, more modern social media sites to use? With social media, you simply post your content and add tags to hopefully grab the attention of potential customers, whereas with email you are on the offense, sending your content directly to the consumer. Social media sites are great for keeping your audience updated and engaged, but email is the hook that brings them in to begin with.

Email is not just a great way to build your audience in the first place, but can also be one of the best options for keeping them engaged and coming back to take advantage of what you have to offer. 81% of shoppers in the United States are more likely to return to a store (either online or in person) because of promotional emails that they either signed up for or received based on previous purchases. Most of these shoppers also state that email is their preferred method of communication with their favorite companies, many of whom enjoy weekly or bi-weekly email promotions (reference 4). Clearly, email marketing is a significant lifeline of today's businesses.

Starting with the Right Software

Maybe it sounds a little strange because of how simple email is to use, but there are different kinds of email marketing software options out there to help you get started. With the right software, things can become much easier, allowing you to automate your email list so that you barely have to lift a finger once the initial setup is complete.

Some options, like MailChimp, will offer a free trial or remain free up until you reach a certain number of contacts on your list, while others, like GetResponse or Remarkety, will have a monthly cost based on the number of contacts you have (i.e. fifteen dollars for one thousand contacts). When choosing the right software for your business, be sure to do some research first - you do not want to end up with software that will actually end up making things more complicated than they need to be. No matter which software you decide to go with, starting a Drip Campaign should be a part of its features.

Drip Campaign Marketing

No matter how hands-on you want to be in regards to

consumer outreach, arguably the best way to go about growing your email list will be with a Drip Campaign, which sends designated content to the subscriber based on a timeline or user action. In a timeline campaign, a new subscriber will receive a new email every few days (depending on the business' preferences) without needing to take further action. The graphic below shows an example of an action-based campaign: the subscriber receives content based on his/her choice. Regardless of which type of campaign is used, each person who subscribes will receive the same content without missing important starter information.

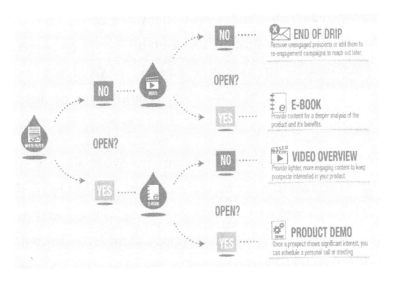

Image courtesy of zapier, What is a Drip Campaign? (reference 5)

How to Build and Grow Your Email List

After picking your software, you are ready to get started building your email list. Be sure to steer clear of bad advice, like using business cards, telemarketing, and bombarding your friends and family about signing up - these methods will not work and will only lead to disappointment and frustration.

A Content Strategy for the Long-Haul

Any big project needs a strategy to make sure that things move forward as planned and lead to the desired outcome, and your email marketing plan is no different. Create an outline for how often you want to release new content and put the plan to action. Creating new content regularly will keep your viewers interested and allow them to see that you mean to stick around and not leave them hanging. This content should be something that applies directly to your target audience. What is even better is creating relevant viral content consistently - you do not want to be a one-hit-wonder.

What constitutes viral content? What about your content will make people want to share it? Firstly, it has to be something that is quick and easy to read. You want to keep your grip on the viewer and stay within the average attention span (which is not very long). Keep your aesthetics pleasing with an easy-to-view color scheme, bold titles, and relevant graphics. Second, viewers are much more likely to share something if it makes them look smart and genuine for doing so. Keep it original, intelligent, and relevant.

Providing a way for the viewer to interact with your content and voice their opinion keeps them feeling involved instead of making them feel like an outsider ingesting information. Try using infographics, calculators, or quizzes to keep your viewers engaged and involved, and keep the content easy enough to comprehend so that they understand what they are forming an opinion on by reading your content.

Everyone Loves Giveaways

Seriously, everyone likes to get things for free - what better way to draw in new subscribers than by giving them a free gift that has to do with your product or service? Creating multiple options (only two or three) to give your new subscribers as a reward is a good way to reach multiple people. We say "multiple" because not everyone will want the same thing; while one person would love your free ebook, another would rather have a video or some kind of product demonstration. Different personalities have different preferences, even within the same demographic. Providing options is a great way to get these different personalities interested in what you have to offer.

Giving out a coupon or discount can work great for pushing your product or service. After all, who does not like getting something for less than what it is worth? Everyone loves a good deal on something, even if it is not necessarily something they were planning on buying. Giving that discount gets attention and increases the likelihood of someone trying out what you are offering. If they like your product or service, they come back - it is as simple as that!

Make Yourself Accessible

Remember, you are the one responsible for putting yourself out there. If you do not reach out to your target audience, how can you expect them to find you and become interested in you? Making your subscription form easy to find is key when trying to build your email list. For a traditional website, your signup form should be in two places: on your navigation bar and in your menu. Placing a link to your signup form right on your navigation bar keeps if front and center, reminding the viewer that they can have access to more of what they are here for with just a couple of clicks. Keeping pages in your menu that your target audience is specifically looking for and adding a link to your signup form somewhere on each of these pages can help to entice the viewer to want more of your content and encourage them to sign up.

For a blog website, you should add a signup form at the end of each of your blog posts. Afterall, if the viewer read all the way to the end of your post, they are obviously interested in what you are offering. You should also include the signup form on your About page, at the footer of your main page, at the top of the sidebar, and in the feature box, as these are all easy-to-see places that your viewers are likely to go to.

Example of an email subscription signup form in the feature box of a blog website.
Image courtesy of SocialTriggers (reference 6)

Your Initial Greeting

Your first impression should be a positive, lasting impression. This means creating a friendly, inviting email response to any new subscriptions, which you will be able to do using your email marketing software. But what should you include in your initial email greeting? The following example is a great place to start:

Hi [Name of Subscriber]
Thanks for joining our email list! My name is [your name], the [creator/founder] of [your business name]. As promised, here is the link to the free [product] you were looking for.
To get to know you better and how we can help you, we want to know

what you are hoping to get from us, no matter how small. Feel free to
shoot us an email to let us know!
Thanks again,
[your name]

Inviting your subscriber to reach out to you and let you know what they are looking for helps them to know that you value them as a customer and are willing to do whatever you can to help them out. It also gives you a better picture of what your target audience wants or needs. Now you know what sort of content you can give them in the future to keep them coming back.

Chapter 3: Getting Started with Social Media

Now that you know the finer details about what you want for your brand you can get started with creating and using social media accounts. Working with social media to launch your brand is based around interaction with consumers, which means focusing on your target audience. Consider which channels of social media your target audience uses most often and are more likely to feel comfortable using to interact with your brand. All social media channels are similar in certain ways, but they are still different and tend to cater to different demographics and psychographics. Picking the right channels to reach your target audience is an important first step in launching your social media accounts and campaigns.

Preparing for Launch

Ultimately, what is the goal you are trying to achieve by using social media? Are you trying to raise awareness among people who have never heard of your brand before? Are you trying to encourage your current fans or followers to learn about a new product or service your brand is producing? The goal in mind should be specific, as should the demographic for your target audience.

Look into what is already happening among your target

audience on social media: what are they talking about? What products and services are they looking for? What sort of information are they sharing with each other? Which questions are they looking for an answer to? Listen to what they are already saying without your brand introducing another topic to them.

Remember that human beings are creatures that respond to emotion; each demographic feels a certain way towards different things. Consider what emotions you can use to your advantage in reaching your target audience and getting the response you are hoping for. What inspires your audience? Which approach can you take to evoke a positive response? Should you use humor, vulnerability, sadness, etc.? Are they looking to be entertained or educated? With these questions in mind, look for a way to incorporate emotion by demonstrating what your product or service is capable of doing for the customer.

You also need to decide which types of content will be received the best by your target audience - videos, photos, articles, and more. When your audience receives your content, how will they respond? You want them to feel a call to action and see the necessity for your product or service. Take your time and do your research. Learn about your target audience so that you can better reach them and waste less time later on.

Branding Strategies

The key to an effective execution is to have a good strategy

- after all, you are fighting against countless competitors out there, and you cannot go about it without a game plan. Remember that you need to stand out, to shine amongst the other brands with products and services vying for the affection of your target audience. So, how are you going to make sure that your brand is well-represented?

The Right Networks

Using the right networks for your outreach goals is crucial to the success of your brand's strategy; even the best brands would fail (or at least not be as successful as they should be) if the wrong social networking tools were being used instead of the right ones. Take a look around and determine which channels best suit your brand's image and work well for the categories that your brand and products/services fall under; you want any advertisements you use via social media to work well, too.

Try not to be tempted to use more platforms than necessary. There are so many options out there, and new ones are popping up all the time. You might think that having an account on every social media platform is the best way to boost awareness, but sometimes less is more. It is better to be good at a small number of things than to be alright at a big number, right? Having a smaller number of social media platforms to work with means having the time and energy to nurture them and maintain them properly. Success using social media to launch your brand takes effort.

We have already talked about doing some research to find out which channels your target audience uses most often and would be the most comfortable using to engage with your brand. After this is done, use the information to narrow down your best options.

Keep in mind that different types of media content work best on different social media platforms. That being said, ask yourself which types of content can effectively convey what you are trying to get across to your audience, as well as which types of content your brand produces well (but do not be afraid of trying new things and pushing your limits). The type of content you will create for your social media accounts will become a big part of your strategies.

Different Strategies for Different Phases

You might only think of creating a strategy for the launch itself, but the time immediately before and immediately after your launch are also great opportunities to build your audience and get people excited about your brand. Sure, the launch itself should be the main event, but anticipation should not be underrated. Think about it: the film industry pumps out multiple movie trailers and teasers a year with the promise, "Coming Soon," knowing that the more people they reach with the teaser, the more people are aware of what they are about to release, and the more likely the theatres will be packed full. Without the initial announcement that your launch is coming soon, you lose a prime opportunity to build up hype and increase the number of potential customers.

The time after your launch is just as important - what good is a great initial launch if it is followed by something mediocre? Build a plan for after your social media accounts are launched and set yourself up for success before you are forced to make decisions about where to go next.

The Face of Your Brand

Social media is largely visual. What this means is that creating visually appealing content is important if you want to keep your audience interested in what you are putting out there. Keeping the look of your different profiles consistent is the base of creating a visually appealing image for your brand and the products and services you are offering your audience. Consistency also allows your audience to easily recognize your brand regardless of which platform they see your content on.

How do you develop visual consistency? Start with an appealing **color palette** that you use in all of your graphics and content, from your logo to your advertisements. With enough exposure, you want your audience to associate these colors with your brand (whether they realize it or not). The best way to go about this is to look at your logo - what colors are present, and which of these are dominant? Stick with these and other colors that compliment your logo. When creating your color palette, remember that different colors have the ability to create different moods and might have a certain impact on how your audience feels about your brand.

Let's look at Coca-Cola as an example: if you go to their social media pages, there is a consistent feel across their Facebook, Instagram, and Twitter profiles. Their color scheme conforms to the style of their red and white logo, creating a consistent feel across the entire page and among their different platforms of choice.

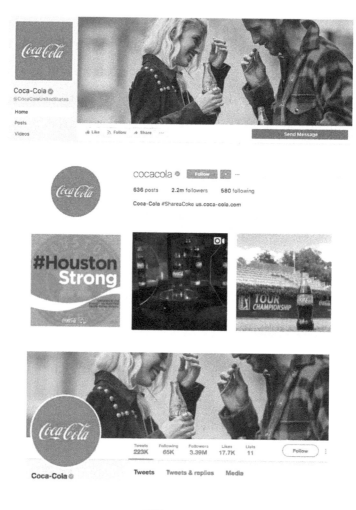

Coca-Cola's Facebook (top), Instagram (middle), and Twitter (bottom) pages.
Images courtesy of Sprout Social (reference #7)

As well as sticking to the same color scheme, you will also notice that Coca-Cola uses the same **logo** as their profile picture in each of their social media profiles. This is an excellent way to keep things consistent, and there is no quicker way to boost recognisability than to put your logo front and center. Of course, Coca-Cola has been around since the 1880s, so even many people outside their target audience will recognize their brand. But even newer viewers are able to recognize Coca-Cola soon after learning of the brand because their consistency makes them easy to remember.

Depending on which social media platforms you deal with, different **filters** are available to change the appearance of your content. While it can be fun to use these filters, you should try to stick to using the same filters for all of your content. Try picking no more than three different filters. Some platforms, like Instagram, will even let you save the filters that you use most or reorder them so that your favorites are placed at the front so that you can skip the search when you go to post something new.

If you are just starting out a small business, you will likely be handling social media yourself or have one person designated to do all of the social media work. Larger businesses, however, can find a social media team to be better when managing their online content. Using **templates** can make keeping the look of your profiles consistent easier. With the use of templates, anyone posting content to your social media profiles is guaranteed to have the right colors and styles to work with, and there is less of a chance of making a mistake. Photoshop (reference 8) and Canva (reference 9) are great tools for creating such templates.

The Voice of Your Brand

The voice that you use to display your brand should be just as appealing to your target audience as the face of your brand. You want your voice - or the way you communicate with your audience - to convey your brand's personality effectively, and finding that voice can take time. Eventually, your brand's voice should become clear and allow your audience to feel comfortable with your brand.

When trying to find the right voice for your brand, consider these three aspects: your business' culture, your target audience, and maintaining authenticity. The **culture** of your business consists of different characteristics, including language, habits, values, and more. So, ask yourself what the culture within your business is. What are your brand's highest values? What makes your brand different or special?

Effective communication with your target **audience** depends on mutual understanding. What sort of lingo is common among your target audience members? You want to connect with your audience, so you should be staying in tune with how they communicate and reach them on their level. You also want your audience to trust you and believe in the **authenticity** of your brand. Fitting in with your audience is great, but not if you have to sacrifice honesty to do so. Your brand's voice should feel genuine and align with what matters most within the business.

Maintaining Consistency

The importance of consistency does not end with the visual part of your brand - the topics that are present in your content should all be relevant to the brand as well. **Topic consistency** can be aided by curating content from other sources, such as social media and relevant websites. Using curated content also brings variety to your social profiles and helps you to avoid getting stuck sending out strictly self-promotional information.

To make sure that you share curated content that aligns with your brand and does not cause confusion to your audience, you can follow topics that relate to your brand on social media. This way, content is placed right in front of you, and you can feel secure about relevance. Your audience follows you because of what your brand is about; you do not want to throw them off by sharing things that they do not care about.

You also want to make sure that your audience does not forget about you because you have not been **posting content regularly**. Sporadic behavior and unpredictability are unappealing characteristics for a brand to develop, and coming up with a schedule for when you should post new content can help to keep you consistent and reliable. The schedule you create will be dependant on the audience you are catering to, and you may have to play around with it a little bit before you really figure out what works best.

Using a scheduling tool such as Later (reference 10) or Sprout Social (reference 11) can make maintaining a posting schedule much easier than if you were to post your content manually. Tools like these can also use analytics to tell you when the best times to post content are, and which types of content get the most attention.

Making the Most of the "Bio" Section

There is something unappealing about seeing an incomplete profile on social media, just like how seeing empty space on a resume gives a bad impression. Take advantage of every space that your chosen social media platforms offer, including the "bio" section of your profiles. This section is exactly where your audience will look to find out what your brand is about and what you do.

Large, well-known brands have the luxury of keeping the content in this section minimal (like including the brand's hashtag), but as a smaller business, you should be using this space to sum up your brand in a few sentences. Do not make the mistake of making a lengthy bio; this is a good way to lose the interest of the reader.

Just as you will use the same profile picture and color scheme for all of your profiles on different platforms, use the same bio for each platform.

Promotion & Engagement

Once your profiles are completed, get some traction by **promoting** them heavily. No one will know about your social media profiles unless you share them, right? Put your profiles out there and invite others to share it as well. If you have business cards, brochures, or anything tangible that you use to reach your audience, include information about your social media profiles to help increase awareness.

You might also need to let those within your business know that you are on social media. A great way to do this is by using an employee engagement tool like Bambu (reference 12), where you can simply send out a message to everyone at once. You can also come up with a pre-written post for each of your employees to share on their own personal profiles as an act of promotion. Your employees are there for the company - use them!

The main uses for social media are to share and to engage with one another. Sharing content without engaging with others does not allow your social media accounts to live up to their full potential. In the beginning when your brand has not yet gotten very much of a following, you can **engage** with others by commenting on relevant posts by other users and sharing your page and content there. You can even engage with competitors as long as it is kept respectful and playful. Engaging with your competitors can play to your benefit, as you make yourself known to their audience as well as your own.

Thinking Ahead

We have already talked about sticking to a few social media platforms instead of jumping into all of them at once. We are not going to go back on that, but it is a good idea to reserve your place on other platforms for later, just in case you decide to give those platforms a try once your initial profiles are succeeding and you are comfortable branching out. Creating an account on other platforms is the best way to make sure that you achieve consistency across all platforms in the name you will be using.

Think about it: you want your name to be the same on every platform so that you are easier to find for your audience. If someone else uses your name before you have a chance to, they can change the reputation of your brand by the content they choose to share. You want your brand to be the first thing that shows up when someone uses Google to search for you, not someone else that has nothing to do with your brand.

Revamping Your Strategies

Even if you have been using social media for your brand for a while now, you might not be getting the results you had hoped for, and it might be time to reevaluate how you go about your social media presence. Maybe you are not standing out quite as much as you were aiming for, or maybe your content just is not reaching your audience like you thought it would. These problems are nothing a little fine-tuning cannot fix.

Show Your Personality

You spent a lot of time on creating a personality for your brand - social media is the place to let it shine! There are things that make your brand different from the others, and those differences are what will make a strong social media profile. You do not want to let the way your profiles function become robotic and lifeless. With the content you post, write your captions and comments in a way that blends with your target audience. Remind them why they follow you!

Social media is not just another way to advertise, but a platform for personal connection. So, let's get personal! It has been shown that story-driven posts and selfies are the types of content that do best on social media. Why? Because they are personal and people can relate to them. Try to make your posts sound less like a business and more like a friend, all the while showing your unique personality.

We all have different opinions, and it is definitely okay for them to be heard. Part of showing your brand's personality would include voicing your opinion. Keep in mind that this should be done with sensitivity and respectfulness kept in mind. Your opinion is part of what makes you stand out, especially if it is different than the majority of other opinions out there.

Add Some "Pop" to Your Photos

Remember when we talked about making your profile

visually appealing through color schemes and filters? The same concept can be applied to the content that you post. You want to be posting things that grab the viewer's attention as they scroll through their newsfeed. Get creative! Use colors and designs that pop out and make the viewer want to keep looking at it.

The use of Subway's colors adds uniqueness to this post.
Image Courtesy of Sprout Social (reference 13)

Like in the image above, eye-catching content can be used to highlight the brand and make their voice heard. Even if there are no photos that work for your product or service, you can add illustrations to an article or post to add a bit of "eye candy" for the viewer.

Tags & Hashtags

Tagging or "mentioning" another social media user in one of your posts ensures that he or she will see your content, as well as putting it in front of the people that follow that user. This is virtually painless, as tagging someone only takes a second and requires no effort. Make sure that the content you are tagging them in is relevant though, otherwise, it can be considered spamming. You can also use **hashtags** to get the attention of anyone who follows those hashtags (again, relevancy is important here). Hashtags allow your content to be searchable, and you can even create your own hashtags for your brand or products and services.

Breaking News

Originality is very popular these days, and that applies to what we see on social media as much as any other aspect of our lives. This can be useful if your brand is conducting original research on a topic, whether you are creating a new statistic, taking surveys, or conducting a case study. Why not break the news through your social media profiles? People love to be the first one to know something new, and providing that new information to your audience will give them something new to share and talk about with their followers and friends. It also allows you to contribute to the conversation in your niche instead of sharing old news time and time again.

Boosting Awareness

Even if things are going well, there is nothing wrong with a little boost now and then. Here are a few ways you can give your viewer count a boost:

- Encourage your followers to share your posts, whether that means retweeting, repinning, or sharing to their profiles

- Create a contest that your followers can enter and/or gain extra entries by sharing your page or content

- Engage more with others by liking, sharing, and commenting on their content

- Create a post in which you ask your audience a question - this will show that you are interested in them, and not just because they like your product

- Share a video where you show your audience how your product or service works or customer testimonials

- Offer your viewers a free demo of your product so that they have the opportunity to try it out before making a commitment

All in all, you will probably have to experiment a little bit in order to get it right, but there is no reason why you should not be able to achieve the awareness you are aiming for when it comes to your brand. Just remember: you want to stick out and be different so that you do not blend in with everyone else. Let the uniqueness of your brand shine through the use of social media!

Chapter 4: Creating a Strong Presence

The general use of social media is completely free to the public - this is perhaps the only feature that the public has been promised will not change by the makers and owners of social media platforms. Regardless of what type of account you set up - whether it be personal or business - your account will always be free of charge. What this means for you is that you have nothing to lose by using it to promote your business (unless you decide to use paid social media advertisements).

When you set up an account for your brand, you have the ability to set your target audience so that your posts will end up directly in front of who you want to see them. You will have to do some work, particularly in the beginning stages of growing your brand's following on social media, by means of being a good advocate for your brand and letting your current customers and the general public know that your brand is on social media. But when the initial groundwork is completed, your brand's social media page will naturally appear as suggestions for users who share interests with your current followers and fall into your set target audience's demographics. Social media provides you with the exact audience you are looking for, even if you decide to expand your target audience to different demographics.

Increasing Your Online Presence

One of the main things you should be thinking about regarding your brand's social media profiles is how to increase your number of followers. The bigger your audience is, the more people will recognize your brand and the greater your chances of converting consumers to your brand. Brand recognition can lead to customer loyalty, which is exactly what you want for the wellbeing of your brand.

Even at the top of your game, there is always room for improvement with how you work with your audience. Always keep in mind who your audience is and how they are likely to change as time goes on. In the previous section, we talked about how to build up your social media profiles and use them to reach your target audience in the most effective ways possible. Next, we will take a look at the different platforms available to you and how to make the most of what they have to offer.

Making the Most of Different Platforms

Among the most popular social media platforms as of January 2018 are Facebook, Youtube, Instagram, Pinterest, Snapchat, LinkedIn, Twitter, and WhatsApp (reference 15). We, however, are only going to focus on a few. Regardless of which platforms you choose to create an account with, you should try your best to gain a good understanding of how it functions and what your audience uses it for before you jump in and make a commitment. You can set up a personal account before creating one for your brand if you would like to take a look around and become comfortable with different features.

Facebook

Facebook allows you to post a variety of content types, like photos, videos, articles, and links. Like we have already discussed, images are the best way to grab the attention of your audience as they scroll through their news feeds. That being said, images should be a regularly used type of media that you share with your followers. More than just for advertising purposes, you can post photos from live events that your business hosts or attends and encourage your followers to tag themselves or people they know. Doing this makes your photos visible to those who follow your followers and expands your audience.

Posting videos on Facebook is becoming more popular, as their effectiveness in reach is increasing. Creating a video specific to your target audience can be more difficult than creating an image, but it can also be worth the effort. Videos are more likely to go viral than photos, and viral content is the exact type of content that you need to help your reach explode.

You can use Facebook's Graph Search to find out which of your existing followers like different businesses and people by searching, "pages liked by people who like my page." This can increase the effectiveness of your marketing efforts if you target the audiences of those pages as well, as there is a chance that the shared interests of your followers can extend to others who like the same things as them. You can also use Facebook Groups to reach your customers in a different way, creating a group that relates to your industry to build closer relationships with your target audience.

Instagram

The main feature on Instagram that grabs viewers and brings them to your content is the use of hashtags. On each post, you can add up to 30 hashtags that relate to the content of your post. Instagram users who follow these hashtags or who search for them will be able to see your content - if they like what they see, the will likely follow you.

It is important to not only rely on hashtags but also create an appropriate caption for your Instagram content. A well-crafted caption can help to increase the engagement of your followers. Captions should only be as long as necessary, considering how they are cut off from visibility after a few lines of text. Including a question in your caption encourages your viewers to engage even more, and inviting them to share your content with others increases your visibility.

A fairly recent addition to Instagram's features is the Story. Even though they are relatively new, hundreds of millions of people view them regularly. Roughly 1 in every 5 stories results in a direct message to the poster, and one-third of the stories that get the most views are posted by businesses (reference 17).

Regardless of whether you are using a regular post or the story feature, consider posting live content. Going live is a good way to grab the attention of your audience, and it encourages them to engage with your content as the post is happening. What is a good example of something you can make into a live post? You can go live when you attend a relevant event, receive a new shipment of your product, or even as your services are being used. Anything can be turned into content for your audience!

LinkedIn

This platform is specifically meant to be used as a networking tool for businesses and professionals. A great way to spread awareness for your brand is to encourage your employees to include your brand on their personal profiles, along with their position within the business. This puts a link to your brand's page directly on the pages of your employees so that anyone who interacts with them and looks through their profile can see with whom they are affiliated and learn more by clicking on the link to your page.

You can search for and join different groups that relate to your brand's industry to grow your network, just like other social media platforms. Join in on the conversation within these groups to connect with other professionals in your industry and share your experiences. Sharing with other professionals increases trust in your brand, which in turn increases awareness and authentic followers of your business.

LinkedIn gives you the option of investing financially in your outreach strategy by promoting your page with advertisements and updates. The ads here target your audience by using different criteria like geography and industry to ensure that your content gets put in front of the right people to grow your viewer base.

Twitter

Using Twitter is almost like attending a networking event from the comfort of your own home or place of business. You can chat with other professionals and put yourself on the radar of potential new followers by using hashtags and mentioning other users, much like Instagram and Facebook.

Twitter allows you to connect with businesses and news sources in your area, as well as those from farther away. If you make connections with local professionals, they are likely to share your content with their followers as you do the same with your own. Building relationships with others in your industry through Twitter is a great way to hear their stories and get some insight about what else you could be doing for your brand.

Tools You Should be Using:

While using social media for your brand is generally straightforward, there are marketing tools out there specifically meant to make it even easier. These tools range from helping you schedule your posts to helping you figure out what content to post and when. They can help you to grow your followers to even greater numbers than by using social media alone.

Canva

First off, Canva is not strictly just for social media. This website allows you to create templates, color schemes, graphics, and more for your brand - it is a particularly useful tool if you find that you have little time to create content for your social media profiles and little to no disposable income to hire someone to do it for you. With Canva, creating content can take a few minutes rather than an hour.

We have already talked about how important it is to include images with your content; Canva is where you can create those images to draw in your audience. From header images to infographics, Canva has a wide variety of templates to choose from depending on what sort of image you are looking to create and which platform you will be posting it on (you can even create your own templates or work without one altogether).

Meet Edgar

If you take a look at some of the most popular brands in your industry, you might notice that their content is used more than once without losing its effect on the audience. This is part of what Meet Edgar does for you - it extends the lifespan of your content by resharing it at times when most of your audience is likely to see it. Edgar also takes a look at the demographics that respond to your content and matches them with more of your content based on category. Essentially, this tool works the same way as an ad would work, except you only have to share the content once and let Edgar do the rest.

This tool is perfect for anyone who is looking for someone else to do most of the work while they direct their efforts elsewhere. Meet Edgar works for different platforms, which means that all you need to do is sync your social media accounts to your Edgar account for your content to be seen everywhere.

Buffer

Before you go out looking at different scheduling tools, take a look at Buffer. With this tool, you can put your marketing strategy on autopilot so that you are not spending hours a week posting content and checking in to see how it is working out. Buffer publishes your content for you depending on when your viewers are most active, allowing you to get the most out of your content.

Feedly

This is a great tool to help with your curated content. With Feedly, you simply search for the people or brands that you would like to see news about and add them to your news feed. In the same way, as your social media feeds, Feedly's news feed will automatically be updated with posts by whoever you have decided to follow. This way, content for you to share as "curated" content comes right to you so that you do not have to go out searching for it.

Feedly allows you to highlight and make notes on anything that interests you so that you do not have to make any changes right away or forget your thoughts about the content. You can also sync your Feedly account with your Buffer account or share what you find directly to your social media profiles.

Followers vs. Customers

Seeing a high number of followers on your social media profiles can be exciting, but remember that you want your hit count to mean something instead of just being a random number. After all, what is the point of having a large following if none of your followers actually buys your product or service? You do not want all of the work you have put into creating your brand and building up your strategy to be for nothing. So, how do you make sure that your followers are genuinely interested in your brand?

Adding the methods that we have already talked about to

your marketing strategy is a good place to start, but there is more that you can do to make sure that your social media profiles are more than just a place to look at something pretty. As we have already discussed, get to know your audience before you put yourself out there. Taking the time to do the research before you launch your profiles will pay off in many ways, including the quality of follower you will attract.

Your audience is more likely to take your product or service seriously if they have a personal relationship with your brand. You can establish a relationship with your followers by responding to comments and direct messages in a friendly and timely manner. Really hone your customer service skills through social media to show your audience that you value their business.

Keep in mind that everyone loves a good deal. Think about how many people will buy something that they would not have considered buying before because it was on sale. Try offering a discount for your product or service or a small gift that is exclusive for your followers to get people to try your brand. If they like what they found, they will likely come back to pay full price later. Contests can work similarly to giveaways, exposing your brand to more people and encouraging your audience to get involved for a chance to win. That being said, you need to make sure that the prize you are giving away is worth whatever is required to enter the contest.

What you want is for your audience to be engaged by your content so that they will feel the need to be engaged with your brand by becoming a customer. Giving your audience the best online experience possible through your social media profiles will help them to see that your business is customer-oriented.

Chapter 5: Rules of Social Media Marketing

Just like every other area of our lives, social media marketing comes with its own set of rules that should be followed if you want it to be done right and see success for your brand. Even though each social media platform has its own unique way of functioning, making your marketing strategy work through these platforms can be done by following the same general rules. In this section, we will take a look at these rules and how to best implement them for your brand to thrive on social media.

The 5:3:2 Rule

One thing you will want to make sure of as you share content on your social media profiles is that you have a good balance of the different categories of content you are putting out there. This is where the 5:3:2 rule comes in: what you post should be fifty percent curated, thirty percent created, and twenty percent humanizing. This ratio has proven to be the most effective way to balance out your content to make sure that you are not just talking about your brand constantly. Your audience wants to know that you care about more than just yourself, and following the 5:3:2 rule is the best way to make that happen.

Curation

Half of your posts should be curated content that is relevant to your brand's industry - that is 5 out of every 10. Looking around for curated content takes a bit of the pressure to create something original off of you and your team. It also helps you to stay up to date on what is happening in your industry outside of your brand. Sharing curated content will show your audience that you care about what is going on around you instead of only being focused on your own business, which is a good quality to have. By seeing your curated content, they will also see that you are not so caught up in your business that you are not aware of what else is happening.

We have discussed curated content in previous sections and its importance to your marketing strategy. Take advantage of the tools available to your business to make finding and creating curated content easier, like Feedly, Storify, Quora, and others.

Creation

For every 10 posts you publish, 3 of them should be original creations. With these posts, you will want to sell your audience on your product or service. Try to avoid going hard here rather than using gentle suggestion to get your point across, as you do not want to push your audience away and see your followers leave. With created content, you can use different types of media, like infographics, videos, blogs, photos, and eBooks. Remember, variety is the spice of life and is more likely to keep your audience interested instead of showing them the same thing again and again.

Humanization

The remaining 2 of your 10 posts should be content that shows the personal side of your brand. This is where you can add a sense of humor or creativity to your brand. Allow your audience to identify with your brand on a personal level by showing them that you care about more than taking their money or becoming the next big thing. This content does not even always have to be directly related to your niche - it can be completely random if that is what works best for you.

Essentials of Social Media Marketing

There are some rules that are very specific to the platform you are using, while others are general and can cover multiple platforms. The rules we will go through here can be followed for such sites as Facebook, SnapChat, Instagram, Pinterest, LinkedIn, and Google+. Regardless of the platform, the general rule that comes before all of the rest is that your audience and remaining personal is key. Social media is about engaging with people on a personal level, and marketing is not exempt from this fact.

Rule #1: Make a Plan

Just in case we have not done enough to drill this home yet, we will say it again: make sure that you **have a plan before you start to act**. Create an outline, do your research, and construct a detailed plan to make sure that you are headed down the right path for what you are hoping to achieve for your brand. You need to have a clear vision for what you are about to do if you want to be met with success.

What should you include in this plan? Right from the start, you need to know the values behind your brand, the important qualities of your product or service, and who you are going to try to reach with your brand's message. Know who you are and why you are doing what you are doing before you turn to focus on your product, and know your product forwards and backwards before you move on to focus on your audience. There is a method to the madness here, so try to fight the urge to rush through it to get to the end. Having structure when executing your plan is important and you do not want it to crumble because you overlooked something.

Rule #2: Build a Strong Foundation

When we talk about building a strong foundation, we are talking about creating **strong social media profiles** to start your brand's outreach. Following the information that we have already covered in the previous sections should help you to build up profiles on whichever platforms you choose to go with. Start by filling out the different sections that each platform outlines for you on your profiles and making sure the information you give is clear and uses words that accurately portray your brand while grabbing the reader's attention. Do not leave any spaces blank as you fill out your profile. Include your logo and your brand's tagline if you have one.

You want your profiles to look professional and creative while **showing your brand's personality** and adding personal touches to show your target audience that you are the right brand for them. Make sure to use the first-person narrative when writing in your information, as this helps to make things sound more personal and less robotic or generic. Use keywords when creating descriptions if you are using Twitter, Pinterest, or Instagram so that you do not fill up the small amount of character space with unnecessary fillers. For platforms like Facebook and LinkedIn, you have a bit more space to talk about who you are, but you should still keep things short and sweet so that your readers will stay interested in what you are saying instead of giving up a few lines in.

Facebook, LinkedIn, and Google+ have the option of creating a **business page**, which is no less important than your profile. You can use this page to provide updates and promotions about your brand to your followers, and share links that lead to your other profiles and websites. This is also a good place to share information about any job openings you might have or start conversations with your followers. In order for the business page to be useful, you need to maintain it, updating regularly and paying attention to any comments or messages that come your way through it.

Rule #3: Connect with Your Peers

Just because other brands and businesses are technically your competition, you can still gain something from **connecting with them as peers**. Social media is the perfect place for networking and making contact with like-minded individuals. Building healthy relationships with others in your industry can greatly benefit your brand as you share tips and experiences with one another as you grow your business and grow your fanbase.

Developing relationships with other brands opens the door to opportunities to **collaborate** with each other, which can do great things for your follower list as you make yourself available to the audience of your collaborators and vice versa. You might also benefit from a mentor-mentee relationship if you reach out to big influencers within your niche. Engaging with competitors in a playful, respectful way through comments and shared posts allows your audience to see that you are not hostile towards other businesses, making you more likable by consumers.

Joining **communities and groups** that relate to your industry opens up the doors to more shared content that you can use, and responding to threads by other users shows your interest in things other than your own brand. When looking for groups to join, look for ones that already have people in them that belong to your target audience - getting involved in groups like this and sharing your content when it is relevant to do so shows these potential followers what you are offering without going directly to them and looking like you are only interested in self-promotion. You can also be a part of **promotional groups** that are specifically meant for sharing content to get promotion from other users and collaborate with others.

Rule #4: Publish Effective Content

We have gone over the different types of content you can post on your social media profiles to pique the interest of your followers in the other sections, so we will not dwell too heavily on it here. As we have already said, **visual content** is the most popular content that will get your audience's attention the easiest. This could be in the form of photos, videos, gifs, infographics, or other images, as long as it relates to your brand or industry.

Whichever type of content you are using, make sure that it is **visually agreeable**; you want to use colors that appeal to the eye and evoke a certain feeling to the viewer. You can use social media tools (as we have already mentioned) to create images with templates and color schemes, such as Canva or Photoshop depending on your preference and experience creating graphics. If you are using an image for a header or title of an article and will be sharing it on different platforms, be sure to use the same image for each platform so that there is a continuous feel for the piece.

You want to provide content that reaches each type of person within your target audience, so do not be afraid to shake things up by sharing a **variety** of topics that appeal to the different demographics that your brand is catering to. In order to give the best possible experience for your followers, you need to understand what is important to them, how they think in general, and how they feel about key concepts. What does your audience respond positively or negatively to, whether that means a type of content, platform preference, or topic?

Keep in mind that different types of content will work better on some platforms than others. You can customize the same content to work nicely on each of your profiles so that no matter which platform your audience is using, you are still getting your message across to them. When adding **keywords**, **hashtags**, and **mentions** on your posts, make sure to use the ones that fit best with the content so that the right people will be directed to your content.

You can share content that you know is already **popular** if you are stuck for something to post. This way, you know you will get a positive response, and in the chance that some of your followers have not already seen it elsewhere, they will come to you first next time because you have already delivered in the past.

Rule #5: Connect with Your Audience

Your audience is the lifeblood of your brand - you do not want to make the mistake of taking them for granted or neglecting them. As your audience comments on your content, make sure that your responses consist of something more than, "that sounds cool," or, "thanks for sharing." **Respond** with questions or personal anecdotes so that your responses have meaning behind them. Responding to comments, questions, and private messages shows that you are willing to actively participate with your followers and want to be in relationship with them. It gives a more personal touch to your brand, which is part of what keeps your followers around.

If you have a specific person in charge of handling social media (or if that person is you), make sure he or she is spending sufficient time per day **interacting** with your brand's audience and provides timely responses to all questions, comments, and concerns that come your way. Your audience needs to know that support is available to them when they need it - no one wants to wait a week to get an answer. In your responses, make sure you are being polite and helpful rather than rude or "salesy." People asking questions are more likely to respond positively if you greet them in a friendly manner.

You can create **communities and groups** within your page for your followers to join based on different topics relating to your brand. These places are great for smaller, more in-depth discussions to get involved with.

Rule #6: Provide Incentives

Sometimes your audience might need a little bit of a push to take a chance on your product or service - and that is completely normal. You can offer **incentives** to show your audience that you have faith in your brand and what you have to offer, which in turn helps them to feel comfortable taking a chance on your brand. You can offer exclusive incentives that are only available to followers on specific channels to increase traffic to those platforms, and you can even make offers that will appeal specifically to certain niches within your audience at different times (after all, it is always exciting when something comes along that is specifically for you, is it not?). Limited-time offers create a sense of urgency to take advantage of whatever it is you are offering, which can also boost traffic during that time period.

Rule #7: Be Generous

Generosity is a good way to increase your brand's popularity among social media users. Being generous can be done in a number of different ways depending on the platform you are using. On Facebook, it could mean sharing posts by non-profits with your friends and followers. On SnapChat, it could mean sharing stories that authentically represent your brand's values to spread the word about what can be done to inspire good in others. On LinkedIn, it could mean giving a recommendation or endorsement to another user to help boost their profile.

Being kind and generous to others on social media can have a great positive impact on those who are following you, as they see that there is more to your brand than self-preservation and "looking out for number one." We should all do our part to help make a difference in the world, no matter how big or small, and trying to make a difference through your brand instead of your own personal image helps to humanize your business. Humanization helps to build trust between you and your audience, and it can be done with little to no effort or sacrifice to yourself.

Rule #8: Expand Your Reach

Once you have settled into your strategy and things are running smoothly, you can work towards expanding your reach and using different platforms more effectively. A good way to make sure that your audience has access to everything you are releasing is to **connect your social media channels** and any other platforms you are using, like blogs or websites. You can use one channel to promote the others with graphics and demonstrational videos to get your audience interested in what else you have out there. This can work for promoting your brand in general as well. Say you have a promotion available on SnapChat - use your Facebook and Instagram profiles to promote your SnapChat profile. Your followers will know that since SnapChat only has content available for a certain amount of time, they will have to act fast to get your offer.

If you have a website created through a platform like

WordPress, you can include **social media buttons** to link all of your social media profiles to your main website - your website acts as an anchor where all of your profiles come together. With one click of these buttons, your viewers are able to access each of your different profiles to reach your content.

Although social media is free to use, you can always give your publicity a boost with the use of paid **promotions** and **advertisements** without pouring too much money into it. By paying a small fee, the platform you have chosen will show your advertisement to social media users outside of your followers based on the demographics of your target audience. Ads and promotions generate more traffic for your profile or page, and the odds of picking up more followers is increased due to the platform's advertising methods.

Rule #9: Analyze and Adjust Your Strategy

Every social media platform comes with its own **analytics** tool to help you keep track of what does and does not seem to be working for your marketing strategy. For example, Facebook has Facebook Insights to track your page or profile traffic and engagement information, and LinkedIn has Company Page Analytics to see your statistics. With the analytics tools provided, you can see which demographics respond to your different types of content so that you can change your methods to better reach your target audience. You can also keep track of what content does best at which time of day and on which platforms.

These tools do all of the heavy lifting and leave you with one job: making a decision on what to change and what to leave the same. You need to give your profiles a fair amount of time before making any judgments, so try out your strategies and track the data for a period of 3 to 6 months at a time. Remember that different strategies will work for different demographics and platforms, and be patient when trying something new. Getting your marketing strategy just right will take time, but your patience will pay off once you have gotten it just right.

Chapter 6: Tactics for Building and Growing Your Audience:

Starting a Like Campaign on Facebook:

If you plan to make use of Facebook at all, you'll want to start by creating a page for your brand. Even if the brand is YOU, you should still create a separate page for yourself. Pages work differently and are formatted differently from personal Facebook profiles. One of the biggest differentiators is "likes." You can't get likes on your personal profile, but you can get as many likes as you want for your brand/company page.

As much as people hate to admit it, they're heavily influenced by the amount of likes something has on facebook. When they see that something is exceedingly popular, they will be intrigued. They will think, this must be important enough to pay attention to. That's how videos go viral on facebook and youtube. Once you get 10's of thousands of views on your video, people that aren't even actively interested in the topic of the video will likely watch it just to see what it's about and how it garnered so many views. This may or may not hold their interest.

Similarly, with brands, people are more trusting and interested in brands that have a big presence. If you're selling T-shirts and you have a facebook page that's linked to your website, people will pay a lot more attention to your page if you have a lot of likes. I'm talking 5,000+. People are wary of brands that don't seem to be popular or don't have much of a social media platform. They think these brands are unreliable or irrelevant.

You might be thinking, that's fine, but how am I going to get to 5000 likes. There a lot of ways to go about this. As with any marketing effort, the harder you work, the more results you'll see. However, for many people, when launching a brand, they may find it effective to create a like campaign. This is a paid advertising technique through Facebook where you advertise through content and paid ads to encourage likes on your page. This can be an extremely effective technique for people who are just starting out and don't have much of a following.

Once you've built up a solid amount of likes, not only will your brand be more credible, but you'll be able to market directly to people who've liked your page and also to their friends. On Facebook, you may often see content in your news feed from a brand's page that you haven't liked yourself. Then you'll see in the notes that several of your friends have liked this brand and that's why it's showing up in your feed in case you also find it interesting.

Using Facebook pixel and Facebooks incredible tools to target a highly specialized audience, you will be able to maximize your ROI and reach people that are most likely to engage with your brand.

For an effective campaign, you'll want to set a goal and a budget as well as a strategy. Here is an example that might help.

Goal: You want to get your T-shirt page from 0-5,000 likes in two weeks.

Budget: You're not sure how much it will cost so you have to experiment for a few days with different settings to see how much these ads will cost you. Once you've fine-tuned it and identified the most effective settings, you can see that a like will average out to about 10-12 cents. Thus, your budget should be about $600 (a small price to pay for the potential payoff).

Strategy: Through split testing and experimenting, you've found the optimal audience and the optimal keywords. You will then strategize how your budget will be spent. You'll set a bidding strategy (it's usually most effective to set automatic bidding so Facebook can optimize it for you), and just set a maximum spend per day. While you're in the testing and tweaking phases, you'll want to set a small budget (less than $15 per day) and once you start getting a feel for what works best, you can increase your budget and launch your two-week like campaign.

Although there are many guides out there to help you get the best ROI for your Facebook advertising campaigns, you have to remember that many of the factors will depend on your brand and desired audience. Therefore, the most effective strategy is often to test out different keywords and demographics and content until you find one that'd delivering the best ROI.

Getting Followers on Instagram:

When just starting out, it can seem so overwhelming. You see so many profiles—people with 10's of thousands of followers and you feel like you won't be able to compete with that. Although building a following takes time and effort, you can quickly exponentially grow your audience both organically and with paid strategy.

You should know that many Instagrammers have "bought" some or all of their followers. There is a huge market out there for buying likes, followers and engagement. This practice is not just restricted to Instagram either, you will find it on Facebook, Twitter, and Youtube as well. Although some people might find this practice distasteful, it can be one of the quickest ways to establish an audience. However, many would argue that your audience won't be very engaged with your brand since you purchased them instead of winning them by attracting and engaging them. It is legal and can help to generate hype around new brands. If you're put off by this idea, you should know that many of your competitors are following this practice and it will be difficult to compete with them.

There are other ways.

Join Instagram Engagement Groups: Finding groups (especially on Facebook) can be a great way to find people interested in your niche. By contributing meaningful content and engaging actively in the group, you will become a valued member and will be able to glean followers from the group—especially from people who have shared interests. It is important to be generous with who you follow as well. Make sure you are also engaging with new members and helping them with their own pages.

Getting Featured: Getting someone else to feature one of your posts or to tag you in their post can go a long way. It will drive traffic and interest to your profile. Of course, similarly, you must be willing to do the same for others. You'll want to be careful with who you feature—their image and message should be relevant to your audience. It should be presented in such a way as something your audience would want to hear—and not just sales pitch.

Consistency: being consistent with your posts and style will attract attention. If people start to know what to expect from you, and it aligns with their interests, they will likely become a follower. However, if your posts are sporadic and all over the board and don't flow, people won't really understand your brand or your influence and won't be drawn to you. Although it may be tempting to post a wide variety of things and focus on a wide variety of content to reach people of many different interests, you will get lost in the crowd. You want to focus on your niche and do it as well as you can as consistently as possible.

Get Influencers: whatever your brand is—whatever your product or service, you need customers. The truth is, people want to hear from your customers. Sometimes, they want to hear from your customers even more than they want to hear from you. They want to hear from a real consumer—someone just like them who has used your brand and has something to say about it. Why do you think people pay so much attention to reviews of products and testimonials? If you can get a few of your best customers to give you a shout-out on Instagram or Facebook or Twitter, or tag you or your brand in their relevant post, you will strengthen your brand and encourage more people to follow you and to engage with your brand.

Follow and Engage with Fans of Your Competitors: many people win followers this way. By identifying who your competitors are, you'll be able to identify people who are actively engaged with them. By following them and engaging with them, they'll often return the favor by following you back or engaging with your brand. On Facebook and Twitter especially, reposting and retweeting the content of influencers and/or questions of people you hope to win over is a great way to boost engagement and increase your followers.

Sharing Awesome Content: This might seem obvious, but many people fail to do this. When sharing content, it shouldn't be all self-promotion. In fact, only a small portion of the content you share should be self-promotion. Especially in the beginning, your audience or potential audience will be wary of you. They haven't become established fans of you and your brand yet. You really want to focus on content that they will find informative, entertaining or at the very least relevant to them. In Digital Marketing, they talk about the 70/20/10 Rule for content marketing. 70% of the time, you should be sharing content that adds value to your audience's lives while simultaneously strengthening and building your brand. 20% of what you post should be others' content. This content can be complementary to your brand or else promoting someone else's brand that doesn't directly compete with yours. As with everything you post, it should be geared towards adding value to the lives of your customers. Keep your sales pitches to an absolute minimum—this is not the time for the hard sell. Content sharing on social media is all about becoming relevant and becoming a valuable contributor. The remaining 10% of what you post can be self-promotional as long as its constructive. This 10% can be strategically sprinkled in amount the other 90% so that people are aware of and interested in your brand's offering, but are not feeling like they're being sold to.

Rapidly Increasing Your YouTube Subscriptions:

There are many people advertising tricks and hacks to get thousands of YouTube subscribers. Most of them are spammy and will get your account banned, but the few that may work in the short-run most likely won't achieve the desired effect. As with most social media marketing efforts, you have to keep your sights always set on the real goal. Your goal isn't just to have a lot of subscribers, your goal is to have a lot of customers. Or even a medium number of very devoted customers. People often mix this up. They opt for the quickest easiest way to a large amount of subscribers, but find diminishing returns. You could get more engagement from 500 true fans, than 10,000 spammy subscribers that you purchased. If you're trying to increase your following and become a social media powerhouse, your goal with youtube should be engagement, views, and growing your fan base. If you have a bunch of "fake" subscribers, or people who aren't actually interested in your brand but whose subscription was purchased, you likely wont get that many views on your videos from your subscribers. A true subscriber will want to watch every video you put out, many of them will like the videos and some will even share them on their personal social media accounts. This is why it's important to establish a true fan base. With YouTube, starting small and growing little by little has proven again and again to be the best way to grow.

Start with People You Already have access to:
Promote, promote and promote some more. Encourage everyone

you know to share and promote your videos. Make them feel like they are brand ambassadors and part of the movement. You can do giveaways and grand prize drawings and have people share your video to qualify.

Promoting is not enough however. Your video has to be quality. Your message has to be important and relevant to the audience you're trying to reach. If you can find ways to reach this audience where they hang out, you will have better success. Get involved in the conversation. Are there Facebook groups? Web Forums? Reddit conversations? Think of any resource you can find where people are having conversations similar to yours and think of creative ways to get them excited about what you have to say. Find ways to get them involved. Make them feel important and part of the discussion. Do not be self-centered and always a self-promoter. You need to show them that you want to provide value to the group as a whole—not just people you know.

The Title is Important: Make your titles searchable. Find the most compelling keywords that apply to your brand and video topic, and put them in your title if at all possible. Be careful because you want your title to be eye-catching and unique without seeming like clickbait or spam. If you cram too many keywords into your title, people will be suspicious and your video may be flagged or removed. Using Google Keyword Planner and websites like BuzzSumo will help you find the most popular keywords in your niche. This may also help you determine trend-worthy topics for your videos and channels if you ever need help with coming up with topics to talk about. You'll want to keep your video under 50 Characters if possible since Youtube will automatically shorten your title for search results anyway.

Customize the Video Thumbnail: Create an image for the Video that creates interest and gives a preview of what the viewer will get once they click on the video. Using large, easy to read text over the image will also help quickly explain to the viewer what they're looking at.

Building Your Audience on Twitter:

Get a Professional and Eye-Catching Profile Picture: if you are a brand and not necessarily associated with one person, you can make your profile picture your logo or something related to your brand. If you are your brand, then you'll want a great, eye-catching photo of you. People like to know who they're dealing with and since Twitter is quite different than Facebook and Instagram in that it's not full of photos of you, this might be one of the few places on twitter where they can see what you or your brand looks like. Under your profile photo, put a statement that says what you want to say about your brand. Include a link to your website, a hashtag if you have one etc. This is where you can differentiate your brand and show people what you stand for in just a few short words.

Be Responsive: By far the best thing you can do to increase your fanbase on twitter is to be responsive. Luckily, this is also the most straight-forward strategy you can employ. Any time anyone tweets at your brand, tags you, uses your hashtag, dm's you etc. respond as quickly as you can. This shows that you care about their interest and that you're there for them. This is an age of instant gratification. People don't want to wait for a response. Often whoever responds quickest gets their business. People want to know that they're dealing with a consistent, efficient and professional brand—this is where you can show them that you are all of those things. Many people make the mistake of taking tweets personally. If someone tweets something negative about your brand or something you don't like, this is not a chance for you to start a twitter war. This is also not a chance for you to make excuses or discredit the complainant. This is your opportunity to take the high road and show everyone how professional your brand is. Address the complaint no matter how rudely it is phrased. Apologize no matter whose fault it is. If there's an opportunity for you to make it up to the unhappy customer or follower, offer it to them. The worst thing you can do here is to make excuses or to argue back. No matter what people might think about the complaint, they will be impressed when they see your professional response. They will think of you as a real brand that cares about their customers and will take care of them. It builds trust in the brand.

Tweet A Lot: this is completely different than Youtube and Facebook and even Instagram. Twitter is all about short frequent messages and content. Posting once a week on twitter wont get you anywhere. Even once a day is not enough. An optimal number of tweets is 15 per day. The good news is that you can automate much of that. Each day or even each week, you can set up all the tweets for the day then schedule them all out so that you don't have to even think about it day to day. That's not to say that you don't have to go on twitter regularly. You should be as responsive as possible to interactions with your followers. The more you post, and the higher the quality of the content you post, the more followers you will get which will lead to more interaction with and interest in your brand.

Pin Your Best Tweets: A tweet that gets a lot of likes and/or retweets that you feel contributes to the strength of your brand can be a great tweet to feature at the top of your feed as a Pinned Tweet. It will catch the attention of newcomers when they see how many likes and retweets you got, and it will also give them an idea of what type of content you curate. This will make them more likely to follow you. Be careful not to pin too many posts and change your pinned posts from time to time. As with al social media, you want to avoid being spammy or gimmicky at all times. Savvy consumers can see right through that and will give you a wide berth.

Chapter 7: Social Media Engagement

While we have talked about building your fanbase and putting your brand's best foot forward on social media, it is important to note that your goal should probably not be to become famous. There are so many celebrities out there, from actors and actresses to reality television stars to Youtube sensations, and achieving attention to the extent of fame is easier than it ever has been before. Even so, trying to achieve fame for your brand can be harder than it looks.

Here is a question to consider: is it better to have millions of followers or a thousand true fans? Followers will like or share your content if it catches their eye, but a true follower will seek out your content and commit to buying your products or services. An article on The Technium (reference 21) defines a true fan as, "a fan that will buy anything you produce," and states that in order to make one hundred thousand dollars per year, you only need one thousand true fans. The idea here is that you would need to make a profit of one hundred dollars per fan (so, one hundred dollars after any fees that it costs you to produce your product or service).

In order to keep true fans, you need to develop a relationship with each and every one of them; learn their names and which products interest them the most, what it is they love about what you are producing, and what they care about in general. Show your fans that you care about them and what they like, and they will be sure to stick around and commit to your brand. You do not need to be famous to be successful - you just need to find your true fans and connect with them.

Finding Your True Fans

Considering the number of people in the world with access to the world wide web, it might be hard to find which of these people will be fans of your work. For all you know, the people that would love to see your content the most live in parts of the world that you are not necessarily targeting through the setup of your social media platforms. There is not a quick and easy way to locate your biggest fans before they know that you exist, unfortunately. Instead of going out and looking for true fans, let them come to you while you do what you can to create relationships with your audience. Of course, there are ways that you can create true fans out of the followers you already have.

If we have not already said it enough, the way to keep your viewers around is to engage with them through commenting and messaging and by creating interesting and interactive content - this takes much more than simply asking someone to "like" your Facebook page. Take a look at the following acronym (reference 23) to get some ideas about successfully engaging your audience.

Ask Questions

Asking a question is arguably the best way to get a

conversation going, but you will want to make sure that the questions you are asking are not conversation stoppers. For example, simply asking someone their name or how they are can only be met with a few short answers. Try asking a question that your audience will want to give details on, like, "What do you think about this?" At least fifty percent of the time, people who spend time online are there to give their opinion on something. Everyone has an opinion, so asking what your audience thinks about an issue or something you have posted is an easy way to get them involved. If you want to get more specific with your questions, go for it!

If you have an email list or are sending out group messages to your audience, ask them for a response. Most emails that you get from businesses specifically say not to respond to the email, but how often do you get one that encourages a response? If that is not enough, try making it a little more personal by specifically saying, "respond to **my** email," instead of, "respond to **our/this** email." Using "my" here humanizes your brand and encourages engagement even more.

You can also ask questions in the form of a poll or trivia game. You can easily create polls on different social media platforms that will make your audience feel involved while at the same time giving you a deeper look at what they think. Trivia questions and personality quizzes have worked for a long time in getting followers to stick around, so why not give them a try?

Encourage Expression

The content that you post is the way you express your brand's personality, so why not encourage expression in your followers as well? Asking the audience to get creative in their responses to your content is a unique way to get to know them and allow them to express themselves, which you do not see everywhere else. You use all sorts of different features to express yourself through your content, like stickers, emojis, audio, filters, and more, so give your audience the chance to do the same.

One way you can do this is through media upload contests, where viewers can create and share their favorite meme, take a unique photo, make a video of their own, or something similar. This can work for drawing/painting, recording audio and video, writing prose, or any sort of creative outlet that can relate to your brand.

A number of social media platforms allow the use of hashtags, so why not encourage expression through this tool? Inviting your audience to add their own hashtags to your content gives them a say and allows them to express what they think of what you are posting. You can also ask for reviews or testimonials of your brand's products or services to let your audience verbally express what they feel about your brand.

Provide Incentives

Including an incentive on your promotions is a great way

to appeal to the competitive side of your audience. You can offer prizes of different sizes or introduce games where the score leads to some sort of bonus. People love games and the opportunity to win something of value, and if including an incentive is going to increase the loyalty of your audience, then it is a win-win for you and your viewers. Make sure when coming up with your incentive that it is something of interest to your target audience that they will actually want to participate for.

Make Offers

Coupons, discounts, membership perks, free shipping, and other offers give your audience a reason to want to sign up to be a regular customer instead of a casual viewer. Different demographics within your audience will want different offers, so play around with which types work best for your following and continue with which ones work the best.

Facebook is particularly good at helping with offer promotion. With Facebook's **offer ads**, your customers can redeem your offer either in-store or online. Make the most of these ads by offering a substantial discount of at least 20 percent, using a set timeframe for the ad to run its course (7 days is an ideal length of time), using an image that will capture the attention of anyone who sees it, and pinning the ad to the top of your page while it runs so that anyone who visits will see it first thing.

Deliver Utility

Along with engaging your audience, the whole point of having interactive content on your social media profiles is to educate the audience. Providing utilities that your target audience can make use of is both helpful and practical. You can use blog posts, infographics, photos, videos, mini-courses, webinars, and other tools to help your viewers and show that you are there for them when they need it.

Exceeding Expectations

Because of its convenience to the user and how quickly things move, social media is easily the most preferred channel by customers when it comes to getting in contact with brands. Consumers have come to expect a certain quality of service, no matter which brands they are dealing with, and will look elsewhere for their needs to be filled if service standards are not up to par.

For example, the majority of consumers that use social media to contact their preferred brands expect to receive a response to their inquiries within four hours of sending them in. In reality, the average response time is about ten hours. Imagine the response of your audience if you not only managed to beat the average but also exceed their expectations for your brand? While it is not possible to track hypotheticals, you can use analytical tools on social media to keep track of different statistics that will let you know which areas you need to improve and the engagement patterns of your audience. We will talk more about analytical tools in the next section.

Build a Strong Team

It might only be you when you first launch your brand, but as things grow and needs become more apparent, you will likely need to build a social media team to make sure that all the bases are covered. Having a strong team of social media experts can help you avoid having customers fall through the cracks and feel like they are not being heard or valued. It can also make the process smoother and less stressful for everyone involved.

There are five different categories to break your social media team into: content creators, community managers, public relations, sales and enablement, and support. Depending on the size and demands of your audience you can group a couple of these together. Your **content creators** are the ones making content to be posted, as well as publishing posts, coming up with ideas, and handling the scheduling tools. **Community managers** will be there to handle big news items and controlling any complicated situations that might arise. Your **public relations** manager's job is to create exposure for your brand and take care of a customer, client, and business relations. Your **sales and enablement** team provides information to customers about your brand and any products or services you offer, as well as promote engagement with anyone who might be interested in your brand. Finally, you need customer **support** to receive any complaints and put out fires as they come up.

Becoming an Engagement Expert

As your brand goes through different stages of its lifespan, always remember the important role that your audience plays. You are bound to face different phases of varying difficulties and find different methods when it comes to content creation or marketing strategies that you will want to try. Do not worry - there is absolutely nothing wrong with that.

Regardless of where you find yourself, engage your audience and work towards meeting the needs of your true fans. Your true fans will be the ones that you can depend on to an extent and that you can base a portion of your strategies around. As the phases that your true fans go through will change, so must you change things about how you relate to and communicate with them.

Chapter 8: Using Analytics to Maximize Efficiency and Guarantee the Biggest ROI

Arguably, there is not much of a point to putting in all this effort if you are not going to keep track of the finer details of your social media marketing strategy. Those details can help you to know exactly what is or is not working for you and what you need to do to make things work better. Every social media platform should come with its own in-house analytics tool built right into the site itself for your convenience. Even if these in-house tools did not exist, there are plenty of other sites that are completely independent of the various social media platforms that can help you to analyze the performance of your marketing efforts and determine the changes that need to be made. How should you be using these tools, and why would you spend your valuable time looking at marketing data when you could be spending it on more important things?

Using Analytics

Any analytical tool that you might use will collect information about your followers, like what they respond to, when they respond most often, and whether their response is positive or negative. Paying attention to this and other information collected can help to guide your marketing strategy to its most effective state. Analytics tools can show which type of content you are posting gets the best results, which platform is working the best for your target audience, and in general, how well you are doing with your marketing efforts.

Specifically, these are the best ways possible that you can use analytics to form your strategy into the best version of itself...

Key Performance Indicators

A key performance indicator (KPI) is a term used to describe the measure that shows how effective a company is at achieving their business's top objectives. You should be aware of what your social media KPIs are before you take a look at your analytics. When coming to a conclusion on what your KPIs are, think about what your business strategy is in general to get a good indication of what they should be (they should be along the same line).

A good analytics tool will be efficient and effective when it comes to identifying and tracking your KPIs. Ideally, the tool you choose will be easy to understand and use. Social media analytics are useful for showing the true value of your social media marketing efforts and using different types of data as leverage for optimizing your social media strategy.

Trend-Based Content Targeting

Any trends that show up online and within social media

should definitely be used to the advantage of your marketing strategy. Social media analytics can be eye-opening when it comes to finding out which types of products, advertisements, or content in general are getting the most interest from not just your target audience, but from other demographics as well. Your goal should be to create content that gets people interested in and excited about your brand, and knowing what else out there is doing so can surely play to your advantage.

Part of your strategy should be staying on top of the difference between how you want consumers to perceive your brand and how they perceive it in reality. The actual perception of your target audience, in particular, can be found out from the "chatter" floating around on social media. You can keep track of what the word is about your brand by searching for keywords and paying attention to the sentiment behind users' comments and the language they use.

Platform-Based Content Targeting

One benefit of knowing and keeping track of your KPIs is that they can help you to target key information on the different social media platforms you use for your brand. Having a strong understanding of the performance of your content on each of your profiles is crucial to the success of your marketing strategy.

Like we mentioned earlier, most of the platforms out there now offer their own analytics tools so that you do not have to go out searching for the right one on your own if you do not want to. Facebook Insights and Twitter Analytics are both examples of native analytics tools.

Personalization

The final area we will discuss when it comes to the usefulness of social media analytics is the personalization of your content and marketing tactics to better match your audience's profiles. Imagine how it would feel to have a brand customize their customer service techniques to meet and anticipate your needs exactly - it would make you feel like you are valued as a customer, would it not?

As already mentioned, creating and posting content by taking a more personal approach and appealing specifically to certain audience members is much more effective than keeping every piece of content generic. Imagine going to a conference and finding that the speakers do not seem to have anything to say that directly applies to you--you would not feel like there was much of a point of attending. But a speaker that hits home with every point that they make would make your attendance well worth the time and money you spent to be there. A personalized experience is always more valuable and beneficial than an impersonal one.

Analytics tools on for social media can help you to create that personalized experience for your entire audience. The data that you find will allow you to find out what content you can and should be creating to be relevant to your followers, ultimately leading to an increase in your ROI.

Tools Available for Social Media Analytics

Other than the analytics tools that come packed in with your social media profiles, what are the other tools that you could be using that might give even more insight into the function of your marketing efforts? The ones we have listed here are just a few of the best ones available to the public, some of which require payment, but all of which are worth looking into depending on your exact marketing needs.

Sprout Social

Sprout Social is good for any brand that uses a variety of platforms, as it works with Facebook, Instagram, LinkedIn, Twitter, and Google+. It allows you to manage each of these platforms from one dashboard to make things easier for you, which also means that you can compare information across each platform in one convenient place. Sprout Social offers a 30-day trial for free before requiring a payment of ninety-nine dollars each month.

Google Analytics

Google Analytics can be used by anyone who uses Google/Chrome as their web browser. Although it is not technically a social media tool, it does offer the ability to track how your social media campaigns are working and measure the ROI of your social media accounts. You can use it to monitor social media use to see the traffic flowing through your different accounts. Because it is built into the Google web browser, it works for any platform that you use for absolutely free. For a similar experience, you could try Adobe Analytics or StarCounter.

Snaplytics

Because of how simple SnapChat is and the minimal functions it offers, it has the least amount of information to offer when it comes to analytics. The range of functions on SnapChat is fairly small when compared to others like Facebook and Twitter; viewing and commenting on content is pretty much the extent of what SnapChat does (which is not a bad thing, just to be clear).

To gather as much data as is possible from SnapChat, you can use a tool like Snaplytics. This tool will take you as deep as you can go, giving you data on things like your snap performances and the growth rate of your audience. It can also give you information about the performance of your Instagram Stories.

There are not a lot of quality options when it comes to SnapChat analytics tools, but you can also try Delmondo and Storyheap if you would prefer to shop around before committing to one particular tool.

Iconosquare

If you want to focus on your Instagram marketing strategy performance, try Iconosquare. Starting at nine dollars a month, you can check your photo, video, and story data, and see influencer analytics for a higher price. Similar to Iconosquare, you can try Later (which we have mentioned in an earlier section as a scheduling tool) or Instagram Insights (the analytics tool that is built into Instagram).

Buzzsumo

Buzzsumo is a little bit different than the other analytics tools in that it examines how your website's content does on social media instead of just how each platform's performance holds up. In other words, it provides a quick and easy way to see how each item on your website does in general instead of having to look at how it does on Facebook, Instagram, Twitter, Pinterest, and LinkedIn (the five platforms it works for). The available plans start at ninety-nine dollars per month - if this seems a little bit too steep for you, you can try Epicbeat or Ahrefs for a similar experience.

Tailwind

Compatible with Instagram and Pinterest, Tailwind is one of the most popular third-party analytics tools out there. It can be used to track your audience count and engagement (among other features), starting at ten dollars per month. If you use Pinterest for the majority of your social media marketing, you will find Tailwind or a similar tool (like Pinterest Analytics or Viralwoot) to be extremely useful.

ShortStack

ShortStack is the perfect tool for a brand that does a lot of contests, as it provides information on how each of your contests performed. Using ShortStack can keep you from accidentally wasting time through contests and help you to make the most of each one that you start. It works for Facebook, Twitter, and Instagram, and is one of the most popular contest tools used. You can use ShortStack for free or sign up for a plan (they start at twenty-nine dollars a month), or you can take a look at Gleam or Woobox, which are comparable to ShortStack.

Squarelovin:

This is a great Instagram app that helps you make the most out of Instagram. It has many useful features but overall, works to help you streamline your Instagram presence and build audience engagement. It helps you find and win over influencers, how to maximize the reach and effectiveness of your content. When used properly, this tool will help you cut the fat on your social media marketing efforts on Instagram. With incredibly insightful reporting, you will be able to see very directly what's working and what isn't and tweak all your campaigns and efforts accordingly.

TapInfluence

The final analytics tool for social media that we will look at is Tapinfluence. This tool is great for any business that uses influencer marketing campaigns, and it works for Facebook, Twitter, Instagram, Pinterest, LinkedIn, and Youtube. You can use Tapinfluence to search for influencers that you might want to work with in the future, or simply to track campaign performance. Alternatively, you could try Traackr or Influency.

No matter which tools you ultimately decide to go with, make sure that they are appropriate for your needs and will benefit your brand the most. There is nothing wrong with trying a few tools out before committing to one. You need to do what is best your brand, and your brand deserves to work at its full potential.

Chapter 9: Paid Ads vs. Content Marketing

We have already covered a lot of information on producing effective content and achieving good awareness levels on your brand's social media profiles through properly exposing said content. In this section, we will attempt to draw parallels between simple content marketing and paid advertisements in order to help you make an informed decision about whether or not paid ads are the right move for your brand.

The use of social media for marketing purposes is a vital part of your brand's marketing strategy overall. Social media is where people spend a lot of time - they log on to communicate with each other, stay updated on events, and learn new things. Not many people will readily admit it, but some folks actually use social media to find out about new products and services that fit well into their lifestyles. Indeed, social media is becoming more and more of a shopping platform. To not take advantage of this pool of potential customers would be a mistake; regardless of what methods you use to advertise on social media platforms, IT NEEDS TO BE DONE.

Both content marketing and paying for advertisements on social media have been proven to help further the success of brands across the world, so no matter what you pick, you should be able to see a positive effect (assuming proper execution, of course). You will simply need to look at the resources available to your brand

and what you cannot do without. For example, what is your total budget for marketing? How many people do you have available to focus on social media, whether that means posting new and recycled content, answering follower inquiries, or sifting through data to better adjust current strategies? Considering the demographics and psychographics of your target audience, how many of your customers follow you on social media compared to other outreach outlets? To be successful in marketing, you need to have a plan.

So, let us take a look at the details of what makes up content marketing and paid social media advertisements.

How Content Marketing Works

Content marketing can be defined as "a strategic marketing approach focused on creating and distributing valuable, and consistent content to attract and retain a clearly defined audience - and, ultimately, to drive profitable customer action." (reference 25). At the very core of your content marketing strategy should be content that is relevant and informative. Being relevant to your audience is a more effective marketing approach than presenting a direct pitch of whatever it is you can offer customers. Throughout this entire eBook so far, we have gone over the different aspects of quality content; by now, you probably know quality content like the back of your hand.

Benefits of Content Marketing

In a nutshell, there are three main benefits of content marketing: cost-effectiveness, an increase in sales, and a higher quality of customer. First and foremost, **content marketing is free**. Instead of spending money on advertising, it can be spent on other things, like production or design. Considering the fact that the average small business spends around one-hundred thousand to one-hundred twenty thousand dollars in a single year on advertising (reference 26), free content marketing looks like a pretty good option.

The most important benefit of this method is that **content marketing increases sales**. The content meant to be a part of content marketing is engaging and real, building trust with viewers and helping them to feel like the brand they are looking at really matters. A relationship is built between the viewer and brand that leads to higher sales than advertisements that jump right into what the product or service is and what it is capable of doing for the viewer. A personal relationship is a better motivator than a product-first approach.

A relationship between the brand and its audience also means that **consumer marketing brings in better customers**. As a result of consumer marketing, you can rest assured that your audience is there for you, not just to have their own needs filled. These customers are more likely to be loyal to your brand as your relationship with them grows, which means that in the event of a mistake made on your end, the customer is more likely to offer forgiveness instead of hostility. A higher quality of customer leads to higher revenues for your business.

Bill Gates once said, "Content is where I expect much of the real money will be made on the Internet." Mr. Gates was right on the mark. The content that you produce for your audience is what they come to your page for - you are kidding yourself if you think they are showing up to see more of your advertisements. Valuable content has the ability to drive audience growth higher than you might imagine.

Drawbacks of Content Marketing

Like everything worth doing, **content marketing takes time**. It cannot be something that you only do once and expect to see great results in the future - you need to continually produce interesting content and promote it in such a way that your audience will be intrigued and move in closer. Making sure that your content is interesting enough to hold your audience's attention takes creativity and patience. Content marketing requires commitment; if you want to see progress, you will likely have to schedule in time that you will specifically commit to carrying out the steps in your content marketing strategy.

Content marketing can feel overwhelming. It requires a well thought-out plan and committed execution of that plan. You can start with an editorial calendar or schedule so that you can see which pieces you plan to publish each week and/or month - you should have at least one month scheduled in advance to avoid getting backed up. Having a specific deadline for marketing can be stressful if you are not used to having strict boundaries in place. The amount of structure needed for content marketing can make paid advertising seem much more appealing.

Building relationships and trust through **content marketing is a long road**. What we mean by this is that you need to have a sufficient amount of convincing content to win over your audience. So, when you add up the time it takes to make all of this content and publish it without bombarding your audience, as well as the time it takes for your audience to go through each piece and let it affect them, you could be looking at many months, or even years, before a viewer becomes a committed customer. This is a long time to wait and work in order to see progress.

One thing to keep in mind when mulling over the pros and cons of content marketing is that everything comes at a cost, whether that cost is financial or another category. Think about what you are willing to go through and what you are and are not willing to give up for the sake of your brand when you are deciding which approach to take for your marketing strategy.

Should You Pay for Advertisements on Social Media?

Honestly, if you are satisfied with the amount of traffic you are getting on your brand's social media profiles, you might not see the need of starting to paying for advertisements. Whether or not you use paid ads is completely up to you - there is no rule that says you have to do it to succeed in your industry. However, you could always be doing more to increase your audience reach, and if you have the funds to pay for social media advertising, then it can be well worth it.

The top reasons that people use social media are (1) to keep in touch with friends and family, (2) to stay caught up on world events, (3) to avoid boredom, and (4) to entertain themselves (reference 27). The most effective paid ads will incorporate one or more of these things to more effectively reach their target audience. Why are these the ads that work? Because they are the ones that do not feel like ads at all. They engage the audience before pushing the selling agenda - the needs of the customer come before the needs of the business on the priority list. Failing to put the customer first when creating paid ads on social media (or anywhere, really), can cause the ads themselves to fail.

What Are Your Options?

One of the first things you will need to decide after committing to paid social media ads is which type of ad you want to try. **Sponsored posts** are posts that are sponsored by a company to boost their viewer count and draw attention to the poster. Essentially, you will pay for this post to get more views by people who are not following you. The platform you are posting on will have tools available for you to use to make sure that your ad is effective. When you post your ad make sure that you select the audience based on your location and that you are sponsoring a post that contains original content about your brand.

Depending on the platform you use, ads show up in different places, like the sidebar or as part of the newsfeed. **Newsfeed ads** appear naturally and fit in with the content already in the user's newsfeed. Having newsfeed ads increases the likelihood of them being shared by viewers, so they are a great way to increase awareness. **Sidebar ads** are located to the left or right of the newsfeed and remain in the same spot as the individual scrolls through their newsfeed. They do not blend in with regular content, so it is much more obvious to the viewer that their purpose is to sell something. Even so, they can be just as effective as newsfeed ads and will likely cost the same.

One perk of paying for social media ads is that some platforms have partnerships with others that allow them to share ads. These **networking ads** allow people on different networks to see your brand and helps to gather interest on platforms that you did not originally post the ad. These ads tend to be cheaper than the other types because they often get clicked on by mistake (it is sort of like getting a discount).

Remember back when we were talking about reusing content to increase the number of views it gets? You can do the same thing with ads with **remarketing**. This ad method redirects your previous site visitors back to your site later on and can double your revenue. Remarketing basically just acts as a reminder to visit your page the next time they use that particular social media platform, so it is a good way to advertise without being too pushy.

The last paid ad type we will mention here is **influencer marketing**. With influencer marketing, you are paying someone with a large following that you would like to piggy-back off of to mention your brand and nudge their own followers to check out your page. If this is the direction you would like to go in rather than paying the social network itself, you should make sure to go about it in a way that will heighten your chances of success. For example, make sure that you choose an influencer that relates to your brand and who has the same target audience as you do. You will also want to pick an influencer who actively engages with their audience rather than just collects followers. Only pick an influencer who gives you a fair price, and consider making creative deals with them such as performance-based bonuses or share-swapping. This method of paid advertising requires a little bit of background between you and the influencer in order to work - pick someone who knows who you are and has already mentioned you in a comment somewhere before trying to make a deal.

SMART Advertising

The goal of paid advertising is always to extend the reach of your brand and boost your profits, but you need a more specific goal if you really want your ads to work. We make goals all the time, and your marketing strategy for your social media profiles can prosper as the result of proper goal-setting.

Think **SMART** when making your goals: specific, measurable, attainable, relevant, and time-bound. (reference 27). Making a goal as **specific** as possible and making sure it is **measurable** means that it will be much more easily achieved, as it will be more effectively kept track of. Any goal you set should be **attainable**, or within reach, so that you are not setting yourself up for failure from the beginning. Keeping your goals **relevant** means keeping small steps towards your goal relevant to the goal itself. For example, if getting more "likes" on Facebook helps you move closer to the goal of increasing social media revenue, it is relevant. And finally, your goal should be **time-bound**, meaning there should be a clear deadline for your goal to be achieved so that you can more easily be kept on track.

Each of the goals you set to move yourself towards the ultimate goal of increasing brand awareness and revenue should fit together like pieces of a puzzle or threads on a tapestry. With your goals in place, planning your strategy in full can be much more simple. You can use tangible methods of keeping track of your goals, like drawing out a timeline for yourself or setting up a small rewards system to keep yourself motivated. It all depends on what works best for you and your business.

Benefits of Paid Ads

Paid social media is the way to go for maximized visibility for your content. The vast majority of social media marketers report an increase in exposure and traffic through their efforts (reference 28). Simply put, the main benefit of paying for advertisements on social media is that you can reach people that you would not be reaching by your own efforts alone. These ads target people based on what they have already shown interest in and the demographics that they belong to. For example, if your brand focuses on selling clothing to pregnant or nursing women, then the algorithm of whichever platform you are advertising on might target social media users who have searched for other maternity or baby products. Regardless of what your brand is offering, there are other brands out there that relate to you enough for you to piggy-back off of their audience.

Platform Ad Services

Facebook is *the* social media platform to use if you are trying to build awareness for your brand. The site accounts for one in every six minutes spent online worldwide, after all. Along with sites like Twitter, Instagram, and Pinterest, Facebook can be used to build awareness for your brand and increase your website traffic. As LinkedIn is more of a brand-to-brand (B2B) networking tool, its focus is more on business networking. That being said, it is also used heavily for increase website traffic and brand awareness.

The Cost of Advertising

Advertising through social media can be relatively

inexpensive - Facebook ads, for example, cost an average of less than eight dollars per mille (thousand impressions). There are different payment options depending on the platform being used - you can pay per mille or per click. Of course, each platform reserves their right to set their own price for advertisements, but they remain fair across the platform range. Consulting with a marketing agency can allow you to make the best decisions for your brand in regards to where you should be spending your advertising budget.

Drawbacks of Paid Ads

Other than the obvious drawback of seeing money leave your company by paying for advertising, there are other drawbacks of paid ads that are specific to each platform (reference 29). While starting up a **Facebook** advertising campaign is easy, affordable, and effective, it can also be time-consuming if you really want it to work to its fullest potential because of the amount of time it takes to monitor their effectiveness. Advertising organically on Facebook seems to be less effective than it once was due to the algorithm changes in their NewsFeed, leading to a higher dependence on paid ads than before.

Instagram can also be considered time-intensive and less effective for organic advertising, and their high focus on images and videos rather than text means that the more textually in-depth content cannot be properly promoted on this platform. They also have a much younger demographic of users, with 90% of them being under the age of 35. Their limited audience reach does not allow for a broad range of brands to effectively use Instagram to promote their products and services.

While it is great for different businesses and professionals to interact with one another, **LinkedIn** has its limits in the educational department; the FAQ and Help sections have considerably fewer resources than bigger platforms like Facebook, leaving something to be desired. In order to get where you want to go on LinkedIn, you need to follow a much more lengthy path and risk getting lost or distracted along the way.

Twitter is perhaps the most limited platform, as messages are forcibly kept brief with a 140 character limit per tweet. Changes to your feed happen rapidly with so many tweets per minute being posted, which means your ads get pushed farther away at a quicker pace than on other platforms. Ads or promoted posts on Twitter are more often viewed as spam, and many brands fail to fit into Twitter's user base.

As you can see, there are going to be certain drawbacks to whichever platform you choose to use for your social media marketing strategy. It is up to you to weigh the benefits and the drawbacks to deciding where it is worth it to spend your hard-earned money when it comes to advertising. To make things a little bit simpler, you can try putting all of the platforms you are considering into a chart so that you can compare their qualities in an easy-to-view format. Do not be afraid to consult with others as well, as they might have insights that you lack.

The Winning Combination

In general, advertising on social media can be a tricky business, even with everything provided to you by the platform. Paid ads can be well worth the time, money, and effort put in, but so can organic content marketing. Ideally, your social media marketing strategy would be a combination of content marketing and paid advertisements. Even with their drawbacks, both of these marketing methods have been proven to boost brand awareness across the different social media platforms and increase customer sales. You cannot go wrong by choosing a strategy that incorporates both paid and unpaid methods.

Let's put it another way...

Think about all of the different ingredients that it takes to make a burger. Some of these ingredients, like cheese, onion, and tomato, are delicious on their own and require very little preparation. Other ingredients, like beef and the bun need to have a bit of work done on them to make sure that they are prepared just right. Combining all of these things together makes an exquisite type of food that you would not be able to imagine turning out the same way if one of the ingredients was missing. Bringing together the cooked beef patty, cheese, ketchup, and other ingredients depending on your taste, creating a satisfying end product.

The same principle applies to creating an effective social media marketing strategy - some components on their own are good, but can be made better by combining them with other crucial components. Paid advertising and content marketing on social media go together like peanut butter and jelly; they are a perfect match and work better together than apart. After you know where you want to go with your marketing strategy, you can find which methods of advertising work best for what your brand has to offer and make a name for yourself.

Conclusion

The average person spends over two hours on social media sites or apps every day. People use social media for communication, education, networking, leisure, and more. It is a great place to stay updated about the things going on in the lives of people around you, as well as current events in your neighborhood, across your country, and even throughout the world. With the amount of time that the majority of people spend online and using social media every day, it only makes sense to use the different platforms available to your brand to market your products and services and grow your business.

During our time together, we have talked about not only the basics of brand building and how to captivate your audience by showcasing your skills and products, but also how to interact with your customers in a way that shows your interest in them both as customers and as individuals. We have learned about the importance of developing a meaningful relationship between your brand and your target audience, and what positive results can follow. We have discussed the different tools available for making your brand's social media accounts stand out among those of your competitors, and the utilities available for the more technical side of marketing. We have covered branding, advertising, networking, and more - everything we could possibly help you with as you aim to get your business off the ground and build up a social media presence from scratch.

Building a brand from the ground up can be a long and arduous process, but what we need to keep in mind is that help is always there if you are looking in the right places. There are countless resources available all over the place, whether you choose to look online or seek the counsel of someone else who has already undergone the processes that are in front of you. Trying to build your business completely out of your own efforts and refusing help can be one of the biggest mistakes you could possibly make.

We want you to succeed in the business world, which is why we cannot stress the importance of an effective social media strategy and positive customer relationships (and even business-to-business relationships) enough. Always remember that your target audience is the lifeblood of your brand; without customers and the needs that they have for your product or service, there would be no point to any of your efforts.

If you follow the guide that we have outlined in this eBook, you will be well on your way to becoming an expert in social media marketing. Remember, any task can be daunting before you have an idea of where to start, but building your understanding of the tasks ahead of you can expel your anxieties and help to propel yourself forward. Do not be afraid to take chances as you build your brand - the rewards that will come out of your efforts will be well worth the risks you took along the way!

References

1.   Statistica, The Statistics Portal. Number of Facebook users by age in the U.S. as of January 2018 (in millions). https://www.statista.com/statistics/398136/us-facebook-user-age-groups/.

2.   Start With Why, Simon Sinek. https://startwithwhy.com/.

3.   Tools Hero. The Golden Circle, Simon Sinek. https://www.toolshero.com/leadership/golden-circle-simon-sinek/.

4.   Mind Tools. SWOT Analysis. https://www.mindtools.com/pages/article/newTMC_05.htm.

5.   Social Triggers. List Building 101. How to Build an Email List... ...And Actually Make Money From It. https://socialtriggers.com/list-building/.

6.   Zapier. What is Drip Marketing? The Complete Guide to Drip Campaigns, Lifecycle Emails, and More. https://zapier.com/learn/email-marketing/drip-marketing-campaign/.

7.   Social Triggers. The 7 High-Converting Places to Add Email Sign-Up Forms to Build Your List. https://socialtriggers.com/email-signup-forms-build-list/.

8.   Sprout Social. 10 Social Media Branding Strategies Every Business Should Follow. https://sproutsocial.com/insights/social-media-branding/.

9.   Photoshop. https://www.photoshop.com/.

10.   Canva. https://www.canva.com/.

11.   Later. https://later.com/.

12.   Sprout Social. https://sproutsocial.com/.

13.   Get Bambu. https://getbambu.com/.

14.   Sprout Social. 12 Ways to Boost Brand Awareness on Social Media. https://sproutsocial.com/insights/brand-awareness/.

15.   Forbes. Which Social Media Platform is the Most Popular in the US? https://www.forbes.com/sites/kevinmurnane/2018/03/03/which-social-media-platform-is-the-most-popular-in-the-us/#5ff080971e4e.

16.   Ad Week. Facebook Hits 40 Million Page Milestone, Launches Live Chat for Businesses. https://www.adweek.com/digital/facebook-hits-40-million-page-milestone-launches-live-chat-for-businesses/.

17.   The UK Domain. How to grow your social media followers to strengthen your brand. https://www.theukdomain.uk/grow-social-media-followers-strengthen-brand/.

18.   Neil Patel. Get More Fans, Followers, and Shares with these 6 Social Media Marketing Tools. https://neilpatel.com/blog/get-fans-followers-shares/.

19.   Quick Sprout. How to Convert Your Social Media Followers Into Customers Effectively. https://www.quicksprout.com/2018/04/04/how-to-convert-your-social-media-following-into-customers-effectively/.

20.   Web Hosting Secrets Revealed. 24 Golden Rules for Social Media Marketers and Bloggers. https://www.webhostingsecretrevealed.net/essential-social-media-marketing-guide/.

21.   KK*. 1,000 True Fans, The Technium. https://kk.org/thetechnium/1000-true-fans/.

22.   Hubspot. 5 Proven Social Media Engagement Strategies for 2018. https://blog.hubspot.com/marketing/proven-social-media-engagement-strategies.

23.   Sprout Social. What Is Social Media Engagement & Why Should I Care? https://sproutsocial.com/insights/what-is-social-media-engagement/.

24.   Sprout Social. 8 of the Best Social Media Analytics Tools of 2018. https://sproutsocial.com/insights/social-media-analytics-tools/.

25.   Content Marketing Institute. What Is Content Marketing? https://contentmarketinginstitute.com/what-is-content-marketing/.

26.   Word Stream, Online Advertising Made Easy. The Comprehensive Guide to Online Advertising Costs. https://www.wordstream.com/blog/ws/2017/07/05/online-advertising-costs.

27.   Lyfe Marketing. Do Paid Social Ads Really Work? You Bet They Do. https://www.lyfemarketing.com/blog/paid-social-ads/.

28.   Blue Corona. Paid Social Media Advertising Campaigns. https://www.bluecorona.com/pay-per-click/social-media-ads.

29.   PPC Hero. Pros and Cons of Top Social Media Advertising Platforms. https://www.ppchero.com/pros-and-cons-of-top-social-media-advertising-platforms/.